AGENDA FOR A POSTWAR
WORLD

Also by J. B. Condliffe

THE RECONSTRUCTION OF WORLD TRADE

A Survey of International Economic Relations

AGENDA
FOR A
POSTWAR WORLD

BY
J. B. CONDLIFFE
PROFESSOR OF ECONOMICS
UNIVERSITY OF CALIFORNIA

PUBLISHERS
W·W·NORTON & COMPANY·INC·
NEW YORK

TO CORDELL HULL

Freedom is recreated year by year,
In hearts wide open on the Godward side,
In souls calm-cadenced as the whirling sphere,
In minds that sway the future like a tide.
No broadest creeds can hold her, and no codes;
She chooses men for her august abodes,
Building them fair and fronting to the dawn.

—James Russell Lowell, "Ode to Freedom"

CONTENTS

ACKNOWLEDGMENTS   13

PREFACE   15

1. A DEMOCRATIC PEACE   27

   The Need for Preparation — The Real Costs
   of War — The Lesson of Past Failures —
   Peace After Victory — A New Balance of
   Power.

2. THE STAGES OF REORGANIZATION   44

   Complexities of a Peace Settlement — A Pe-
   riod of Economic Transition — The Danger
   of Postwar Inflation — From War to Peace
   Collaboration.

3. THE POLITICAL BASIS OF ECONOMIC
   CO-OPERATION   62

   The Power of the United Nations — Region-
   alism in Europe — Regionalism in the Far East
   — The Limits of Regionalism — International
   Economic Co-operation.

4. THE MEANING OF SOCIAL SECURITY   85

   Insecurity of Restrictive Nationalism — The
   Need for Adaptation — Maintenance of Em-
   ployment — Essentials of Social Security —
   Co-ordination of Credit Policies.

7

8   CONTENTS

5. THE DISPOSAL OF AGRICULTURAL SURPLUSES   102

A Continuing Crisis — Accumulation of New Surpluses — International Commodity Controls — The Ultimate Causes of Disequilibrium — German Agrarian Protection — Protection of High-cost Agriculture — Need for Improved Nutrition.

6. DEBT AND DEMOBILIZATION   132

The Lessons of Mobilization — The Greater Difficulty of Demobilization — Planning for Postwar Employment — Co-ordination of National Policies.

7. REPAYMENT AND REPARATION   150

The Legacy of World War I — Lease-Lend Indebtedness — The Problem of Reparation.

8. INTERNATIONAL ECONOMIC DEVELOPMENT   167

New Frontiers of Investment — Raising Consumption Levels — New Forms of Investment — Mistakes after World War I — The Importance of Technical Aid — Refugee Settlement.

9. THE DILEMMA OF COMMERCIAL POLICY   189

Access to Raw Materials — The Spread of Economic Nationalism — Transitional Controls — British and American Policy.

CONTENTS   9

10. LONG-RUN OBJECTIVES   207

     Wartime Centralization — Cautious Relaxa-
     tion of Controls — A World Safe for Bu-
     reaucracy — Dangers of Regulated Trade —
     Exchange Stability.

11. ILLUSION AND REALITY   223

INDEX   229

LIST OF ILLUSTRATIONS

FIGURE   PAGE

1. CENTRAL AND EASTERN EUROPE IN 1815   68

2. CENTRAL AND EASTERN EUROPE IN 1914   69

3. CENTRAL AND EASTERN EUROPE IN THE 1920's   71

4. SOUTHEASTERN ASIA   75

5. COMPOSITE INDICES OF STOCKS AND PRICES OF PRINCIPAL AGRICULTURAL COMMODITIES, 1923-1939   104

6. ANNUAL AVERAGE PRICES OF IMPORTED AND DOMESTIC WHEAT IN EUROPE (UNITED STATES PRE-DEVALUATION GOLD CENTS PER BUSHEL)   120

ACKNOWLEDGMENTS

THE genesis of this book was a study submitted to the American Section of the Committee for Economic Reconstruction of the International Chamber of Commerce, under the chairmanship of Mr. Thomas J. Watson. The author wishes to express his thanks for permission to make use of this study in the present volume, which is published on his own personal responsibility. He is deeply grateful also for the searching criticisms of an advisory group of economists, under the chairmanship of Professor James T. Shotwell, called to advise the American Section of the Committee, working in concert with the Carnegie Endowment for International Peace. Individual acknowledgment to members of this group might seem to commit them to agreement in detail which the author has no right to assume; but special acknowledgment is due to Professor Shotwell, without whose help and encouragement the book would not have been written.

Imperfect as it is, this formulation of the issues of postwar policy could not have been attempted but for the generous help the author has received in recent years from economists in many countries who have collaborated with him in the studies of trade regulation sponsored by the Rockefeller Foundation.

J. B. C.

PREFACE

THIS book is an attempt to set out some of the intricate, vast, and fundamental issues that must be faced in any attempt to establish a lasting peace when this war ends in total defeat of the totalitarian aggressors.

In this preliminary outline of problems and policies, attention is confined largely to certain economic aspects of the immediate postwar situation. The pattern of probable economic needs and possibilities for action, when the war ends, can perhaps be foreseen somewhat more clearly than the political forces that will then be operative. Impoverishment, industrial dislocation, and inflation are already well advanced in many countries. It may be that these processes of economic disintegration are already inescapable or may become inescapable because of untoward political developments. The manner in which an attempt may be made to grapple with them clearly depends upon the social and political attitudes of those who will have the power to act. The guess may be ventured, however, that the realities of a desperate situation may give little scope for doctrinaire advocacy of free enterprise or socialist planning. If effective action is to be taken quickly enough to cope with the immediate postwar situation, it must use the agencies that are available. These will be primarily the co-operative agencies developed by the United Nations in pursuance of their joint war effort.

If emphasis has been placed upon immediate postwar problems, and primarily upon their economic aspects, this is not in ignorance of the ferment of social and political change that is likely to transform the postwar world. The chapters that follow raise many far-reaching issues, but do not deal with many others of even wider scope.

There is no discussion of colonies, to take one example. It seems obvious enough that the nineteenth-century colonial system, by which a small group of western European countries developed great colonial areas primarily as sources of cheap food stuffs and raw materials, is challenged and may not long survive this war. Some powers have been unable to hold and develop their colonial territories in competition with other imperial states. Moreover, the growing nationalism of the colonial and semicolonial areas must be reckoned with. Japanese industrial development, even when distorted by militarist aims, has been an object lesson to the world. Territorial imperialism, annexing colonial territories outright, is one way to link industrially advanced and backward peoples. A truly international administration of undeveloped territories as "a sacred trust of civilization" is the real alternative to such imperialism. The mandate system, as it was actually administered, proved neither one nor the other, and its failure has been tragically demonstrated in the Pacific, where the democracies are paying a bitter price for their share in crippling its possibilities. Further steps toward self-government will certainly be taken in many areas. The problem of the weaker colonial peoples is more difficult to solve.

To organize an international colonial administration takes time. Moreover, the flagrant betrayal of trust and the treacherous use of diplomatic privileges by Axis nationals have left bitter memories and a profound reluctance to trust them again as collaborators in international organization.

Such problems are left aside in this book, together with many controversial questions of long-run social and economic policy. The emphasis is on more immediate issues. Whether truly international institutions can be organized, whether free capitalist enterprise is likely to survive the great expansion of government initiative caused by the war—these are questions that might be debated at length. But there can be little doubt of the prolongation of wartime procedures and mechanisms into the demobilization period just after the war. To suggest ways in which these procedures may be directed toward laying the foundations of a co-operative and expanding prosperity is the main purpose of this book.

Necessarily, the major responsibility for laying down the principles of a peace settlement is assumed to rest upon the United Nations. No one can foresee which among the United Nations or who in the United States will be the most powerful arbiters of the peace that is yet to come. But it seems certain that the influence of the United States will be important if not predominant. History has shown that executive decision cannot effectively commit the United States in great policy issues. In a democratic country, such issues must be settled by the sovereign will of the people. If they are to be understood they must be widely discussed and debated beforehand.

It is as a contribution to such discussion that this book has been written. Its title indicates its purpose. It lists what must be done if a co-operative postwar world is to be created. The issues with which it deals are controversial, but not confidential. They do not impinge upon strategy. No military secrets are involved in discussing them. Political aims are so involved; but in a democracy, political aims ought not to be secret. The aims upon which this agenda is postulated are those stated in the official pronouncements of the administration and notably in the joint statement of the President and the British Prime Minister as a result of their Atlantic Conference. The proposals made are intended to suggest for discussion practical ways by which those aims may be achieved. They have no authority beyond whatever logic may be inherent in their presentation, and they draw upon no material that is not accessible to any diligent student. They commit no responsible organization, and all of their suggestions are open to criticism and discussion.

Two obvious objections may be raised to such discussion at the present time.

The first arises from the fear that discussion of postwar problems may detract from concentration on the supreme necessity of first winning the war. To achieve victory entails a mobilization of resources greater than has yet been attempted, or perhaps even visualized. Any softening of the will to win is to be deplored. But in modern war, the definition of aims is itself an important weapon. It is indeed an essential weapon in a democratic community.

The second objection arises from the scope and revolutionary character of the present conflict. This is a strange war following unforeseen patterns with unforeseeable consequences. The length of time needed to achieve victory is an obvious factor bearing upon the potentialities of reconstruction. It has recently been said that no formula can yet be advanced for reorganization after victory because all the terms of the equation are unknown. It is true that political, economic, and social institutions have been shaken as never before. It is equally true that much depends upon not only when, but how victory is finally achieved. A successful Russian resistance and counter-attack which were the chief means of sapping and then breaking German military power would, for example, create a situation very different, particularly in Europe, from that which might result from victory brought about, after severe Russian defeats, largely by American production if not by American armed force.

To plan in detail, however, is not the object of this agenda. Such plans must wait upon events and in any case can be made only by those who have access to detailed official, and often secret, information. To raise broad questions of principle upon which decisions must be taken before detailed plans can be considered, much less put into effect, is an entirely different matter. It is not too soon to raise such questions if their import is to be the subject of democratic debate and discussion. Unless there is such debate and discussion, the sovereign will of the people cannot be enlisted in effective support of a workable, co-operative plan for a peaceful world.

It is common knowledge that serious discussion has already proceeded in official circles in London, Moscow, and Washington concerning the principles and even some of the details of a future peace. Consultations between the United Nations have at least begun. Even more important, actual collaboration in the conduct of economic policies, collaboration that can hardly terminate abruptly when hostilities end, has gone a considerable way. The situation, indeed, can be stated simply. The totalitarian governments pursued policies in peace that prepared for war. The United Nations are bound, on the contrary, to pursue war policies that will prepare the machinery of peace. They are already a great comity of nations pursuing common aims. The machinery they devise will be the only machinery available for international action when the war ends.

This book, therefore, has been written on certain definite assumptions. The first, obviously, is the assumption of victory by the United Nations; such a victory as will free them both from the necessity of adapting the free democratic countries to conformity with totalitarian ideas, and from the equally unpleasant necessity of matching a "New Order" in Europe and Asia, and indeed in the whole world outside of the United States.

The shape of the Nazi New Order is already clear.[1] It is a carnivorous order seeking whom it may devour. The only possible way to live in the same world with it is to grow protective armor, remain within the confines of defense and even then exercise eternal vigilance. Hitler's New Order, according to its exponents,

"offers unity for anarchy; a simplified currency; a vast and homogeneous territory, unbroken by irrelevant frontiers, within which enterprise can deploy unimpeded its energies; the rational vigor of a planned economic system superseding the squalid scramble of petty national rivalries. All customs barriers in Europe would be abolished.

[1] *See*, for example, Thomas Reveille, *The Spoil of Europe* (New York, 1941).

The monetary system would be based on an index of the value of individual currencies in relation to the German mark. The Reich, as the greatest continental state, would control all European economies, would rationally and justly distribute all capital goods, and would allot to each nation certain special tasks." [2]

But this unity would be a unity of submission; the enterprise and rational vigor would be German, and the justice and rationality with which capital goods are distributed and tasks alloted would be determined by the arbitrary will of the dominant conqueror and not by any known rules of law. [3]

The second assumption is that there can be no real hope of staving off chaotic upheavals in the postwar emergency, unless the most powerful of the democracies takes its share of leadership and continuing responsibility. The United States has more power and influence in international affairs than any other nation.

[2] R. H. Tawney, *Why Britain Fights* (London, 1941), pp. 21–2.
[3] *Cf.* Douglas Miller, *You Can't Do Business with Hitler* (New York, 1941), pp. 6–7: "What has happened is the fact that the individual has no basic civil rights now. German courts are instructed to decide cases not purely upon written law, but according to 'healthy public opinion.' Since such opinion is not recorded anywhere, this means in practice the judge's opinion at the time, and the judge is a Nazi functionary. No firm or individual has any rights which the government is bound to respect."
The demand made by Hitler for reaffirmation of his arbitrary powers and his sharp criticism of the judiciary, in his speech to the Reichstag on April 26, 1942, merely emphasize the point made above. The powers were of course reaffirmed by unanimous vote of the Reichstag: indeed no opportunity was given for a negative vote to be registered.

To many of its citizens, the responsibility that goes
with such power is both unsought and unwelcome;
but it is inescapable.[4] What the United States does
will largely determine the pattern of international
relations for the immediate future. Even inaction is
a policy, negative but nonetheless decisive.

The third assumption follows naturally. The United
States is a democratic country. No one can count upon
the desires of its executive officers being implemented
by effective action unless the "folks back home" un-
derstand and approve the broad principles upon which
executive action is based. The division of powers
between the judicial, executive, and legislative
branches of the government is expressly designed to
ensure that ultimate decision rests in the hands of the
sovereign people. The best-laid expert plans drawn
up in Washington will go awry unless they are backed
by popular understanding and support. To secure that
understanding and support involves a great campaign
of public education and debate.

Berkeley   J. B. C.

[4] *Cf.* Edmund Burke, *Thoughts on the Cause of the Present Discontents:* "Public life is a situation of power and energy; he tres-
passes against his duty who goes to sleep upon his watch, as well
as he that goes over to the enemy."

"Yet much remains
To conquer still; Peace hath her victories
No less renowned than War; new foes arise
Threatening to bind our souls with secular chains."

JOHN MILTON, *Sonnet to the Lord General Cromwell*

CHAPTER I

A DEMOCRATIC PEACE

The Need for Preparation

EVEN before the United States was attacked by Japan and was thereby forced into open war against all the Axis powers, the war was of such a size and moved so rapidly that its battles were named by countries or oceans; the battle of Poland, the battle of Britain, the battle of Russia, the battle of the Atlantic. It has now become a global war.

The strategy of total war on a world scale was projected by the totalitarian leaders. Their challenge has been accepted. As these lines are being written, the opponents of totalitarianism, the United Nations, are developing the strategy of their great alliance. Henceforth, the war will be waged, as the Seven Years' War was waged, on frontiers all over the world as well as at home, but this time with modern weapons and masses of force. To keep the fighting men supplied with the tools of modern war involves economic mobilization and effort on the greatest scale.

At such a time, when to underestimate the foe or neglect any corner of the vast battleground is to risk ultimate and total defeat, talk of peace or of the problems it will bring is often discouraged. The war must first be won. Economic warfare rather than economic co-operation preoccupies the minds of those in authority. In the conduct of that warfare, social well-being must be subordinate to war production. Strategy takes precedence of trade. Preventive buying of raw materials, blockade, subsidies and loans, the freezing of foreign funds, and bilateral purchasing agreements become prime instruments of policy. The object of the war alliances is not to promote international co-operation for the enhancement of economic prosperity, but to mobilize military resources, and in so doing to cripple the enemy.

But in fact the peace will come out of the war, and its preparation is a part of the democratic war effort, as well as the end for which the war is being fought. It is indeed unlikely that either the war or the peace will be won unless the foundations of a freer postwar world are laid in the course of fighting the war. Effective mobilization of the free peoples demands action, now, that will make the United Nations the working nucleus of co-operation in the postwar world. To wait till peace breaks out before making plans for the postwar world is to invite defeat of the nobler purposes for which the United Nations are fighting. If it is true that "peace hath her victories," it is equally true that peace can have resounding defeats. As in war, the main cause of such defeats is unpreparedness.

The greater part of this book is concerned with problems likely to arise in the difficult years of transition, when national economies geared to war must be changed over to production for a peacetime world. After this war, the peace must be politically hard, but it ought to be economically generous. Such a peace at the close of such a war means that some crucial decisions must be taken very rapidly. Arbitrary and swift action will almost certainly be necessary to avert a chaotic collapse of all organized social activity in many stricken countries. Troops of occupation must be flown to strategic centers to keep order, and to control (so far as may be) the blood bath of vengeance that is threatened. There must also be prompt action to avert starvation and a complete stoppage of industry in countries—including enemy countries as well as those now in enemy occupation—where all resources have been thrown into desperate total war or have been destroyed in its final frenzy. At the same time competent economic experts should be assigned to survey monetary and budgetary problems in their relation to the real economic needs of these countries. It is too late to check inflation when the printing presses are already rolling. Reconstruction after inflation is both more painful and more difficult than timely measures to prevent the disorganization that is symbolized by budgets and monetary systems getting out of control. The sooner a comprehensive plan of controlled adjustment to the new conditions can be put into effect, the easier it will be to avoid the economic and financial disasters that followed the last war. National action is needed, but it cannot be counted on in this respect. Piecemeal measures are costly and inefficient.

The experts sent in to survey the financial situation and economic needs of various countries should be chosen from an international panel and be responsible to constituted international authority. They should make a bold, comprehensive plan and make it quickly. Relief should be a demonstration for, and the means of organizing, the kind of world the United Nations want to create. Relief officials, who will be the saviors of many peoples, should not go down in history as great philanthropists, but should be the servants and visible embodiments of a better world order. Their courage and character, the expertness of their staffs, and the vitality they may bring to exhausted and broken communities should derive from and build toward a free order, offering butter for guns, and democratic freedom, as preferable to militarist tyranny. Above all, they should aim at encouraging self-help, at controlling panic, and averting despair. To feed the hungry and heal the sick are noble aims, but the best way to achieve them is to restore self-respect, to get people back to work, and revive their faith in social order.

In the same way it would seem clear that political decision should be rapid, clear-cut, and backed by authority. Effective government ought to be sustained or restored as quickly as possible. It would be fatal to al-

low prolonged wrangling and bickering over boundaries or other political questions. Compared with the
dangers of social disintegration, such matters must be
regarded in their true perspective. Important as they
are, it is more important to preserve the structure of
government and orderly co-operative social processes.
At the close of the war, the main principles of political
settlement should be laid down. They ought to be
worked out in advance. Procedures and institutions
for adjustment of detail might well be created at the
same time. It is, indeed, less important that the peace
should be just than that it should be adjustable. There
should this time be reality in Article XIX of the League
Covenant, a workable and working mechanism of
peaceful change and growth.[1] But it would be highly
dangerous to the world economy, and therefore to political stability, if there should ensue a long period of
discussion and intrigue in a so-called "armistice period."

The Real Costs of War

On the other hand, it is not possible to work either
political or economic miracles by a stroke of the pen.
Millions of men and women are now engaged in the

[1] "The Assembly may from time to time advise the reconsidera-
tion by Members of the League of treaties which have become in-
applicable and the consideration of international conditions whose
continuance might endanger the peace of the world." League of
Nations, *Official Journal*, Vol. I, No. 1 (February, 1920), p. 8.

fighting and supply services. The whole mechanism of economic life is organized for war. It is not possible easily or suddenly to dismantle munitions plants, erect civilian factories, transform the production and distribution of goods and services, release price and production controls and rationing priorities, and bring budgets back into balance again. It is possible, however, to prearrange prompt and determined action designed to maintain political order, and to establish machinery to grapple with emergencies and facilitate an orderly transition to peacetime economy.

The difficulties of the change-over from war to peace should not be underestimated. The costs of war are real. Material destruction is the least of them. The damage done to the immaterial nervous mechanisms of social co-operation is vastly more significant. There is no magic formula by which these real costs of war can be exorcised. The return to peace will involve painful sacrifices and difficult economic adjustments. On the other hand, there is no reason to accept as inevitable a vast and calamitous disorganization of economic, financial, and monetary co-operation. A sober and realistic view would not expect peace to bring a millennial world of economic harmony and higher consumption levels; but it need not anticipate chaotic disorder.[2] A sober and realistic program would seek to prevent wild budgetary and monetary inflation, but in so doing, it would seek also to avoid a deflationary panic. It would

[2] Cf. P. Horsfall, "Some Doubts as to the Imminence of the Millennium" in *World Order Papers*, first series (London, 1940).

accept the necessity for prolonged effort, for adjustment of production costs, and for difficult sacrifices by sectional vested interests; but it would not abandon the national economies to ruthless competitive readjustments and rapidly falling prices leading to cumulative deflation.

It ought to be possible by concerted and prearranged planning to keep firm political control of the immediate postwar situation, and at the same time to arrange procedures for a comparatively orderly transition to peace production. Given a measure of political stability and co-operative international arrangements, it should be possible to work out positive monetary and fiscal policies, especially in the United States and Great Britain, designed first to check the danger of an inflationary boom and at a somewhat later stage to prevent a deflationary slump.

Such policies would facilitate the very considerable adaptations of prices and costs that will be necessary to restore a workable and balanced equilibrium between national industries, and between national economies, on a peacetime basis. Government action should be designed to hasten rather than postpone such adaptations to economic realities. In particular, it should be directed toward increasing rather than hampering the mobility of labor and capital. Instead of sustaining employment and production in the war-stimulated industries, every effort should be made to develop them in the industries needed for peace.

Such a combination of monetary and fiscal policy,

price-cost adjustment, and improved mobility will not be easy to achieve. It may be that the best to be hoped for is the prevention of major disasters, such as uncontrollable inflation in some areas and drastic deflationary unemployment in others. But an effort should be made to create the monetary and fiscal conditions in which capital and labor can move as quickly and painlessly as possible, and without violent dislocation, toward a new economic equilibrium adapted to peace rather than war. Only by such an effort, concerted as far as possible on an international scale, can further disaster be avoided.

If international co-operation designed to control inflation and forestall unemployment cannot be achieved, there will almost certainly be a period of intensified and restrictive economic nationalism in which the effort to protect each national economy will ensure the ruin of all. Much of the following argument is predicated on the necessity of avoiding resort to ruinous tariffs, currency depreciation, and other policies of competitive economic nationalism. It is a delusion that nations can protect themselves, much less gain, at the expense of others.

The Lesson of Past Failures

In the years before 1939 many powerful agencies, public and private, strove unceasingly to settle political

issues and restore co-operative economic relations between the great trading nations of the modern world.
In retrospect, the utter failure of those efforts reads
like the inevitable progress of a Greek tragedy in which
the nemesis of an inescapable doom brushes aside puny
mortal efforts to avert disaster. One impasse led to another. Statesmen turned from their failure to establish
some effective form of collective security to negotiate
regional pacts, thence to disarmament discussions, and
then back again to collective security.

In the economic field there was a similar turning
from one expedient to another.

"The difficulties encountered in abolishing import and
export prohibitions in general led to an endeavor to
concentrate on certain specific products. The unsatisfactory results of strictly limited negotiations led back
to the idea of a general concerted action, to be initiated
by a tariff truce. Repeated failures on the world plane
suggested the idea of the apparently less ambitious
scheme of a union purely European. More recently and
more generally, the discouragement engendered by the
impossibility of securing any measure of significant
agreement by means of multilateral conventions has
caused most governments to fall back on the time-
honored but far more modest form of bilateral treaties." [3]

Such experiences, repeated in many fields, suggest the
futility and frustration of a caged animal incessantly
seeking some new or old avenue of escape.

[3] William E. Rappard, *Post-War Efforts for Freer Trade* (Geneva, 1938).

This was not for lack of expert technical knowledge and practical plans of action. The record of the years between the wars is strewn with expert suggestions and plans, such as those of the Economic and Financial Organization of the League of Nations and the International Labor Office. Powerful private bodies, such as the International Chamber of Commerce, drew upon the best expert knowledge of the whole world in the formulation of such plans. In the summer of 1936, for example, the International Chamber of Commerce, in collaboration with the Carnegie Endowment for International Peace, published two significant volumes traversing the whole field of international economic collaboration.[4]

A glance through these and similar studies is sufficient to show that ways and means could have been found, and alternative practical plans were in fact suggested, whereby the rapid march toward economic disintegration might have been arrested. Scientific knowledge and economic enterprise could have been directed toward the enhancement of social well-being instead of being mobilized for destruction. The tragedy was not inescapable. The cause of breakdown has not been any external problem, such as "a loss of command over the human environment." It has lain in the failure to enlist for peace and constructive co-operation the

[4] *International Economic Reconstruction: An Economists' and Businessmen's Survey of the Main Problems of Today;* and *The Improvement of Commercial Relations between Nations* (Paris, 1936).

resolute common will and patriotic readiness to accept sectional sacrifices which every nation can enlist for war.[5] Wrong decisions of national policy, particularly by the great nations, have been taken: not for lack of expert knowledge or practical warnings, but because the issues were imperfectly understood, and because the immediate risks and costs loomed too large in the minds of those responsible for such decisions. In part the failure is one of leadership; but in large part also it is a failure of public opinion in the great democratic countries.[6] Too many statesmen and businessmen have taken the short rather than the long view, preferring to hope that temporary solutions might stave off the ultimate disaster.

There were, it is true, skillful and courageous policies of adaptation in particular countries, and there were periods when international equilibrium appeared pos-

[5] *Cf.* the passage from George Meredith, cited by Arnold J. Toynbee, *A Study of History*, Vol. IV, p. 120:

> "In tragic life, God wot,
> No villain need be! Passions spin the plot:
> We are betrayed by what is false within."

[6] *Cf.* R. H. Tawney, *Why Britain Fights* (London, 1941). "A piercing vision is the gift of the gods; but the road to hell is well supplied with signposts, and we can, at least, refuse to run in blinkers. As far as the majority of us are concerned, it is blinkers—first passion, as in 1919; then amiable, thoughtless complacency, as in the fatal decade after that; then a resolute refusal to see brutal facts, for fear of the responsibilities that, if seen, they might involve— which have done most of the mischief of the last twenty years. . . . It is possible that not the least guilty among the authors of war were those of us who desired only to be let alone to live in peace."

sible. But no general international agreement could be reached, and without such agreement the best-planned national efforts were limited in their possibilities. The economic causes of war are often exaggerated. Political causes are far more important. But the failure to achieve international economic co-operation in the years between the wars opened the way for political factors to operate. The greatest responsibility for that failure must devolve upon the great trading nations who were unwilling to adapt their economies as international necessity demanded.

Peace After Victory

These reflections on the errors of the immediate past throw much needed light on the troubled present. It is only too easy now, when every nerve must be strained to mobilize economic resources in a life-and-death struggle, to accept the view that conflict is natural and inevitable, and that peaceful co-operation is a visionary dream. Indeed, it was precisely because great nations had accepted that view that conflict became inevitable.

No economic historian is likely to overlook the successive mistakes and the failures to realize international co-operation in the years when shortsighted policies continued the last war into an uneasy peace. The disillusion and frustration of those years provided the opportunity for militarist-minded groups to seize power in Italy, Germany, and Japan. But if the democracies have some responsibility for the conditions that put these militarist groups into power, the acknowledgment of their responsibility should not obscure the all-important fact that those groups, once they were in power, rejected co-operative procedures and prepared for conquest. This rejection constitutes a challenge to the very fundamentals of international economic co-operation. The totalitarian governments do not seek to evade or disguise this fact, but glory in it. They have set out, in the words of Hitler, to ensure that the world "will be ruled by the laws of force, when the people of brutal determination, not those who show self-restraint, will triumph." In these circumstances, however they came about, those who believe in and strive for international co-operation in the economic as in other spheres have no option but to accept the totalitarian challenge.

It is little wonder that expert knowledge and technical economic plans were abortive in the years immediately preceding the war. Not economic welfare but military power was the aim of totalitarian economic policy. There could be no possibility of international co-operation when great powers did not want to co-operate, and when they rejected as unworthy the very notion of co-operation except on their own terms of conquest and domination. There can be no effective plans for reconstruction until this issue is settled. What follows, therefore, is not in any sense a project for a negotiated peace. There can be no peace between these warring ideas.

Acceptance of these necessities of the present situation does not, however, entail abandonment of the ideal of international collaboration and action. Such abandonment would itself be defeat, since it would mean acceptance of the false philosophy against which the bitter struggle is being waged. It is true that in time of war effective action requires the relinquishment of certain privileges that are cherished in the piping times of peace. But it is equally true that the pattern of peace is woven during the war. To postpone plans for reorganization until the emergency of peace is upon us is to invite disaster.

As Mr. R. H. Tawney has well said:

"To suppose that our victory will close all accounts is to deceive ourselves. The crisis confronting the world is not a mere interlude from which it can turn, when the last bomb has been dropped, to re-knit, with a sigh of relief, the broken threads of its existence. It is part of a process of disintegration long at work beneath the surface, which unless we arrest it, will continue in peace as well as in war, and for which the victors, not less than the vanquished, will pay a heavy price. Our first duty is to hold the gates of freedom open against the tyrants who would close them. Our second duty is equally plain. It is to clothe freedom with the positive significance which belongs to it only when it means, not the mere absence of restrictions, but the presence of opportunities by which all can participate, according to their powers, in the treasures of civilization." [7]

[7] R. H. Tawney, *op. cit.*

A New Balance of Power

It is obvious that new and unpredictable factors will enter into the settlement after this war. In the Far East, China will have the opportunity to become a great power, while Japan will be broken. India, for good or ill, will achieve political independence. The colonial system in southeastern Asia can hardly revert to its nineteenth-century tradition. In Europe, the long struggle between Slav and Teuton will end this round with the power and prestige of the U.S.S.R. greatly enhanced. The frontiers of the U.S.S.R. may be redrawn. Independent new Soviet Republics may well emerge in central and eastern and even western Europe. The influence of a U.S.S.R., which has met and broken the assault of the Nazi armies and their satellites, will be powerful in the creation of the postwar world order.

It may be that the suspicions and fears that in the past have been barriers to co-operation between the democratic peoples and the U.S.S.R. will be modified by their intimate collaboration in the course of this war. Such a healing process, involving a considerable effort of understanding and changed policies on both sides, would ease the problems of reorganization when the war ends. The nineteenth century was colored by the American and French Revolutions which were essentially assertions of individual freedom and individual rights. The twentieth century is likely to reflect the

influence of the Soviet Revolution which was fundamentally an assertion of social control over individual
privilege. It is true that the fear of Jacobinism that
haunted Europe after the terror in France was laid
when dynastic government was restored in 1815,
whereas the revolutionary government has strengthened its power in the U.S.S.R. Improved relations
between that government and the Western World,
therefore, depend largely upon the moderation of its
unofficial revolutionary connections abroad and upon
greater understanding in foreign countries of its fundamental purposes and achievements.

An even more difficult educational task to be ac-
complished will be the effort to reintegrate the peoples
of Germany, Italy, and Japan, who have acquiesced
in and supported the policies of aggression that have
challenged the very bases of civilized co-operation.

The main purpose of this book, however, is to ex-
amine a more immediate task confronting the democratic peoples, and especially the United States. The
United Nations dare not rest content with winning this
war. Unless they take up, and carry through, the task
of devising a form of world order in which aggression
clearly will not pay, the war will probably have to be
fought again. The aggressors have come close to winning this war. If there is another war a generation
hence, they may come closer still.

In a decent society, crime does not pay, but this is
only because good citizens realize that they dare not

allow potential criminals to delude themselves that it does. The responsibilities and duties of world citizenship in this respect have been imperfectly realized by the great democratic peoples. The war will have been fought in vain unless those responsibilities and duties are taken more seriously for the future.

CHAPTER II

THE STAGES OF
REORGANIZATION

Complexities of a Peace Settlement

AFTER previous wars peace has generally been concluded by a formal treaty, following which normal diplomatic and international economic relations have been resumed. There has been a "peace settlement." The major issues of conflict, such as boundaries, have been agreed upon, or dictated by the victor, and international co-operation has been restored, within a new political framework but upon the old pattern.

It may be, however, that the treaties which embodied the "settlement" after the war of 1914–18 will prove to be the last of their species. Total war is as much revolution as war. It hurls into battle not only military force, but the whole apparatus of government and organized social life. When it ends there may be difficulty in finding a responsible government with which to negotiate peace, let alone work out continuing methods of international co-operation.

Already the question arises in the most practical forms: With what German government will the

United Nations be prepared to treat and on what basis? Will they treat with any? Or must Germany be occupied and governed till some acceptable alternative to National Socialist government arises? Will the boundaries of the U.S.S.R. be enlarged, in the east, in the southeast, in the west, in the northwest? Will the United Nations recognize independent, new Soviet Republics if those arise in central and southern Europe, or in France or Germany? Will the governments now in exile be restored to power in the territories from which they have been driven? Will the boundaries of those territories be restored as of September, 1939? Can the same principle be applied both to homogeneous, well-defined areas, such as Belgium, Holland, and Norway, and also to Czechoslovakia, Poland, the Baltic States, Finland, and the Balkans? Will it apply in Asia and Africa as in Europe, to Manchukuo as well as to China south of the wall? Will Korea regain its independence?

If, as a measure of practical necessity, the governments in exile are restored to power so that there may be some means of prompt and effective action in their former territories, will they be able to command the allegiance of their nationals who have endured the Nazi occupation? Will their recognition by the United Nations depend upon the popular support they can command? Will full and unfettered national sovereignty be restored to them? Or will stipulations be made concerning regional federations and the pursuance of co-operative economic policies? Will their powers be derived from and supported by a new international authority or by the victorious coalition of great powers? Can certain functions of sovereignty be reserved as more appropriate for international than for national decision? [1] Can the restored sovereignty be made conditional upon the relinquishment of these functions to an appropriate international authority? Or would it be more practical to rest content with the partial achievement of the purposes aimed at by forming customs unions in regional areas?

Such questions as these might easily be multiplied. They are clearly relevant to the solution of the very intricate and baffling problems of commercial policy with which the postwar world will surely be faced. It is not possible to project lines of international agreement concerning tariffs, quotas, exchange control, monetary policy, exchange stabilization, access to raw materials, the disposal of agricultural surpluses, shipping, price and production controls, social security, public works, and reconstruction schemes unless there is prior decision as to the units of government among

---

[1] *Cf.* R. H. Tawney, *op. cit.*, pp. 24–5: "It is obvious, in the first place, that a wide range of subjects has hitherto been regarded as the exclusive sphere of national governments which, in the circumstances of today, cannot properly be so treated, and that a drastic revision is required of the respective provinces of national and international authorities. Commercial policy, including tariffs; currency and credit; migration; through communications; the command of the key-points of commercial intercourse; the control of international combines and *kartells*, are matters of general, not particular concern."

which such agreements may possibly be negotiated. Something more is said later concerning the political aspects of these economic problems. They are mentioned here solely to make the point that it would be unrealistic to imagine that, after this war, a final peace settlement can be negotiated in a brief space of time between established and fully responsible governments.

A Period of Economic Transition

Indeed, the problem is more complex than is apparent from the fact that new governments must be created, possibly in areas differing from the prewar state boundaries and with more restricted functions than those formerly exercised by sovereign states. In every war, there occur great distortions of the productive mechanism and heavy strains upon the immaterial but vital co-operative processes typified by monetary and credit relationships within and between national communities. After the last war the foundations of national credit were so badly sapped that mounting budgetary deficits led to uncontrollable inflation in a great many of the vanquished countries. Much more is at stake in the present war, since there have been revolutionary changes in the control of credit, in the organization of production, including labor, in the exchange of goods and services, and in the regulation of all external commercial and financial transactions, including debt payments, tourist traffic, and other invisible items as well as commodity trade.

Some understanding of the problems that are created when industry is regulated for war purposes may be gained from the reaction to the first severe rationing of materials used in the production of automobiles in the United States. In addition to problems of re-equipment and employment at the manufacturing end of the industry, there arose at once "grave alarm at the thought of the wreckage of a distribution system that would have to be reconstructed from the ground up before the automobile industry could begin a postwar recovery." [2] In countries where for many years, even before the war, private industry has been totally subordinated to military production, such wreckage is likely to be widespread and thorough.

It is the sheerest folly to imagine that international co-operation along prewar lines can be immediately restored with countries whose international connections have been destroyed. One cannot co-operate with a void. This was abundantly proved by the virtually complete collapse of trade with Russia after the last war. If the restoration of trade with continental Europe after this war is attempted solely by the methods of private industry, the Russian experience may well be repeated.

It should be obvious, therefore, that a period of economic transition must be envisaged. While it is clearly

[2] "No More Automobiles," *Fortune* (November, 1941), p. 196.

desirable to shorten the period of political confusion and uncertainty when the war ends and to establish effective government as quickly as possible, it is equally clear that the machinery of long-term peaceful collaboration can be put together only gradually, and in the course of dealing with urgent emergency problems.[3] Indeed, the sense of historical continuity which is developing is wider and deeper than this brief statement might suggest. It is increasingly realized that the pattern of possible international collaboration for the future is being determined now, by the measures being taken to organize collaboration for war purposes among the United Nations.[4]

The Danger of Postwar Inflation

It may be recalled that the Supreme Economic Council found itself charged with such tasks at the close of

[3] Cf. Quincy Wright, *Political Conditions of the Period of Transition* (mimeographed), Commission to Study the Organization of Peace (New York, November, 1941).

[4] Cf. e. g., Report of the Eighth Fortune Round Table on "Peace Aims" (held at Princeton, February, 1941), p. 18. "At the end of the present war we believe the task of reconstruction should be entrusted—not to a hurriedly convened peace conference—but to the organs already developed by the Democratic Bloc during the present war. What we envisage is a continuing organism—a kind of permanent negotiating body—to sweep away the debris of the present war and lay economic and political foundations for the future. The United States, in particular, should continue to participate in the Democratic Bloc during the demobilization period, which may last five years or more."

the last war; but inter-Allied collaboration broke down before the first postwar economic crisis, and the United States had retired from effective participation in European affairs before the period of uncontrollable inflation.[5] The warning recently given by Professor Staley on this point is, therefore, very timely.[6]

"One need not (he points out) anticipate a prolonged period of so-called 'economic exhaustion' in the world. The productive power of the modern economy is enormous and if it can be kept working at anything like full capacity the world may be surprised at the speed with which wartime destruction can be made up. The problem of retransferring soldiers and munitions workers to peacetime employment may also produce some surprises, especially for those who think that immediately after the war there is likely to be a great wave of unemployment. In actual fact, the United States and other countries not devastated by invasion or disorganized by defeat are likely to experience a boom and a labor shortage rather than unemployment for a year or two immediately following the war. This will be because of the large

[5] Cf. H. W. V. Temperley, *A History of the Peace Conference at Paris* (Oxford, 1920); Frank M. Surface and Raymond L. Bland, *American Food in the World War and Reconstruction Period* (Stanford, 1931); and N. B. Dearle, *Dictionary of Official Wartime Organizations* (London, 1928). For a concise discussion of these events *see* Henry B. Brodie and Karl W. Kapp, *The Breakdown of Inter-Allied Economic Collaboration in 1919* in National Planning Association, *United States' Cooperation with British Nations*, Planning Pamphlets, No. 6 (August, 1941).

[6] Eugene Staley, *The Economic Aftermath of the War*, Commission to Study the Organization of Peace (New York, October, 1941), mimeographed.

pent-up demand for durable consumer's goods and for replacement of equipment, the result of doing without during the war. In fact it may be necessary to continue some of the wartime controls in order to prevent this sudden release of demand from producing inflationary price rises and dangerous temporary overexpansion of certain peacetime industries. After the pent-up demands have been satisfied—that is perhaps eighteen months or two years after the end of the war rather than at once —then the real danger of a disastrous slump and unemployment will occur. It is important to be clear about this. If we anticipate, falsely, that there will be mass unemployment immediately after the war and that soldiers and munitions workers will be long out of jobs, a temporary boom may throw us off our guard. Just as we are settling down to normalcy the real troubles may begin—like the explosion of an unsuspected time-bomb."

This warning, it may be noted, does not contradict, but supplements, the argument that it may prove very difficult to establish co-operative economic relations with the beaten totalitarian countries. Professor Staley is writing more specifically of conditions in the United States. It is probable that the void in Europe will be bridged by emergency organization in the immediate postwar period. If it is not, the countries short of materials may not have any postwar boom. Austria did not after the last war, but passed straight from postwar penury into the chaos of inflation. This raises at once a more delicate and difficult problem: Is Germany to be included among the "countries liberated from

Nazi oppression" for which reprovisioning plans are now being made? If she is so included, her economic disintegration may perhaps be avoided.

Material shortages and damages can be quite quickly repaired. The main ingredient of the "unsuspected time-bomb," however, is precisely the immaterial damage to monetary, credit, and financial relationships on which stress has been laid earlier. It should be remembered that after the last war there was not merely one but a series of delayed credit explosions. The immediate boom and slump in 1919–20 were in fact much less serious than the later crises from 1929 to 1933.

The immediate task of emergency relief, though urgent and complex, is less difficult and less likely to be neglected than the subtle and intricate problem of bracing strained currencies and overburdened financial systems against the painful readjustments and reckonings that will be necessitated by any return to a flexible and mutual balancing of international payments. The fact that readjustments and reckonings may be somewhat delayed reinforces the argument that emergency procedures in the transitional period ought to grow out of, but make a decisive break with, the methods of wartime collaboration and lead in turn to more enduring mechanisms of permanent collaboration.

From War to Peace Collaboration

Official negotiations looking toward such an evolutionary procedure have already begun. The President of the United States and the Prime Minister of Great Britain, in their Atlantic meeting in August, 1941, made known "certain common principles in the national policies of their respective countries on which they base their hopes for a better future for the world." Of the eight principles briefly enunciated, three—the fourth, fifth, and seventh—deal specifically with international economic problems.[7]

On September 24, 1941, representatives of eleven Allied governments,[8] meeting in London, took note of the Atlantic Charter, declared their adherence to the common principles of policy there set forth and their intention to co-operate to the best of their ability in making them effective. In pursuance of this intention they stated five principles of action culminating in the establishment of an organization "by His Majesty's Government in the United Kingdom" with which the Allied governments and authorities would collabo-

[7] *See* Chapter III of this book, p. 64, where the Charter text is quoted.

[8] "The United Kingdom, Belgium, Czechoslovakia, Greece, Luxembourg, the Netherlands, Norway, Poland, U.S.S.R., Yugoslavia, and the representatives of General de Gaulle, leader of Free Frenchmen."

rate.[9] The bureau thus established, it is true, has its
function defined somewhat narrowly in terms of the
emergency that is expected to arise immediately at the
conclusion of hostilities. Its main purpose is "to secure
that supplies of food, raw materials, and articles of
prime necessity should be made available for the postwar needs of the countries liberated from Nazi oppression."

The interest both of the United States and of the
British Dominions in this immediate task and in the
long-run problems of economic reorganization is obvious. This interest is inherent in the role which the
United States is playing in the war as the main arsenal
of the United Nations, in the procedures by which
financial and material aid is being given to the other
embattled democracies, and in the provisions ultimately
to be made for the settlement of accounts.[10] No better
illustration need be asked of the way in which war
policies are inevitably being projected into the future
peace.

A shrewd European observer has recently stated the
situation plainly:

"By Congressional enactment, the President of the
United States, whoever he may be, has been given power

[9] "Allies Chart Post-War Plans," *The Inter-Allied Review*, No. 9
(October 15, 1941).
[10] The Secretary of State and the Secretary of Agriculture have
announced the willingness of the United States to co-operate. Cf.
New York Times (September 25 and 26, 1941).

no human being has yet been vested with in modern history; namely, he, and he alone, is to determine what, in his judgment, should be the counterpart that the democracies fighting today should tender to the United States in exchange for aid of all kinds that they will be receiving now on an ever-increasing scale.

"That presupposes—and we are witnessing it every week—closer and closer collaboration in the planning of economic and financial strategy that will cover the period of the war and the period after the war. In the hands of the British Commonwealth, its lesser overseas allies, and the United States, in their control, there rests today the wealth of the globe, outside the European continent, as well as the predominant means of industrial and agricultural production and the entire financial resources of the world. It is the administration of this real wealth, the wealth to produce goods and render services, that will be the determining factor in shaping the transitional period." [11]

If the machinery of wartime collaboration is examined more closely, however, it becomes obvious that it is by no means safe to assume either that collaboration will continue after the war emergency is past, or that the machinery devised for war purposes will prove adequate for the different purposes and conditions of peace. "We must not be too easily impressed by the mere numbers and complexity of the agencies and

[11] *Cf.* Dr. L. Rajchmann in *The World's Destiny and the United States: A Conference of Experts in International Relations* (Chicago, 1941), pp. 65–6.

procedures which are now in operation nor by the volume of their work." [12]

The scope of present collaboration between the United Nations embraces a great number of the problems of economic co-operation that will arise in a different (and often reverse) form after the war. It is important to realize that

"those responsible for governmental action during the emergency have been inventing methods for day-to-day collaboration on (1) shipping and shipbuilding, (2) the transfer of war materials and food, (3) the standardization of military equipment, (4) military strategy and intelligence, (5) exchange controls, (6) the transfer of capital assets, (7) the freezing of funds, export controls, pre-emptive buying and other problems of 'economic warfare,' and (8) the exchange of civilian defense information and advice." [13]

But it is equally important to realize the improvised character of the methods invented. There has been a confusion of changing relationships among the war agencies and the older departments of government. That confusion has reacted upon business and public opinion. The lack of clearly defined channels of authoritative decision and of adequately staffed organs of over-all planning, competent to devise policies leading to "unity and balance" in the very complex fields

[12] Planning Pamphlets, No. 6, pp. 4–5. Cf. also, to the same effect, Eugene Staley, *Wartime and Peacetime Economic Collaboration* (Princeton, September, 1941).
[13] *Ibid.*, p. 4.

of endeavor that are involved, was for long months a serious defect. The problem of administrative machinery is still not wholly solved, even in regard to the war effort.

In the United States, national planning of domestic policies for the postwar period is distributed over various departments as well as the National Resources Planning Board. Many departmental agencies are involved in activities outside the United States, but ultimate decision rests with the State Department. Final decision on the economic, as all other, aspects of international relations is in the hands of the Department of State whose powers under the Constitution have been reaffirmed on two recent occasions. The Economic Defense Board (now the Board of Economic Warfare), created by executive order on July 30, 1941, is actually practicing international collaboration in the prosecution of economic warfare. Its powers and authority in this respect have been greatly strengthened by the reorganization of government agencies effected in April, 1942.[14] Its mandate is drawn in the widest possible terms, particularly in the field of international economic relations.[15] But that mandate is primarily for

[14] *Cf.* Department of State Bulletin (April 18, 1942), Vol. VI, No. 147, Publication 1731, for the executive order effecting this organization, and *ibid*. (May 2, 1942), p. 6, for a supplementary Presidential statement affirming the ultimate authority of the State Department.

[15] "The conduct in the interests of national defense, of international economic activities, including those relating to exports, imports, the acquisition and disposition of materials and com-

the organization of economic war. The transformation of these various agencies into an effective organ for the promotion of peacetime collaboration demands not only effective prior planning, but the exercise of positive executive authority at the critical moment. That authority necessarily resides in the President of the United States.

It is true that economic collaboration among the Axis powers suffers from even greater preoccupation with war aims. It is, indeed, designed to continue the war organization permanently. The Axis machinery creaks even more ominously than that of the United Nations. Defeat for the Axis would thoroughly disrupt and discredit the so-called New Order and its instruments. On the other hand, it may be expected that the United Nations' machinery which has won the war will be consolidated and have enormous prestige throughout the world.

The French proposals, in 1918, for the continuance of international economic collaboration, were in effect proposals to continue co-operative economic warfare

---

modities from foreign countries, including preclusive buying, transactions in foreign exchange and foreign-owned or foreign-controlled property, international investments and extensions of credit, shipping and transportation of goods among countries, the international aspects of patents, international communications pertaining to commerce and other foreign economic matters." The Board shall "make investigations and advise the President on the relationship of economic defense measures to post-war economic reconstruction and on the steps to be taken to protect the trade position of the United States and to expedite the establishment of sound, peacetime international economic relationships."

into the peace.[16] The French leaders, it must be said, had a clearer view of the political realities than did the British or Americans. They pleaded consistently against reliance on formulas and word magic. In their view, the only guarantees of peace were either an economic (and therefore military) domination of Germany or else effective measures to enforce collective security by creating an international force. M. Clémentel's proposals referred to above were in the first category.

It is improbable that similar proposals can be effectively revived after the present war, and improper that they should be. Economic policy after the war will demand the provision of equal access to raw materials rather than preclusive buying; the freeing as opposed to the freezing of exchange assets, the expansion of multilateral instead of the canalization of bilateral trade, the promotion of foreign investment in place of capital transfers to pay for war materials, and measures to sustain rather than restrain purchasing power. These are all the reverse of present objectives, and it is not likely that they can be achieved by the same methods.[17]

[16] Cf. H. W. V. Temperley, op. cit.; Surface and Bland, op. cit.; and Etienne Clémentel, "La France et la politique inter-alliée," in Histoire économique et sociale de la guerre mondiale (Série française), Publications de la Dotation Carnegie, pour la paix internationale (Paris-New Haven, 1931). The whole series of volumes comprising the Economic and Social History of the World War contains valuable material on the problems discussed in this book.

[17] Cf. Annual Report of the Bank for International Settlements (June, 1941), pp. 191–92.

In the relief of the war's ending and because of the opportunities for quick profit that a replenishment boom may offer, there may be widespread impatience and heavy pressures from powerful interests eager to get rid of wartime controls. Such pressures were potent both in Britain and in the United States after 1918.[18] They offer ample scope for disagreement among the collaborating nations. Even before the Armistice was signed, on November 7, 1918, Mr. Hoover, in his official capacity as United States Food Administrator, cabled his representatives in London a flat veto on "any program that even looks like Inter-Allied control of our economic resources after peace." [19] The reasons he gave derived not so much from any belief in economic individualism as from distrust of Allied motives and their probable behavior. That the possibilities of such mistrust being revived are not negligible is obvi-

[18] Cf. Sir William Beveridge, British Food Control (New Haven, 1928), Chapter XIII, "The Battle of Decontrol," for a reasoned discussion of the case for abolishing the controls of food production and prices.

[19] Planning Pamphlets, No. 6, p. 44: "For your general advice, this government will not agree to any program that even looks like Inter-Allied control of our economic resources after peace. After peace, over one-half of the whole export food supplies of the world will come from the United States and for the buyers of these supplies to sit in majority in dictation to us as to prices and distribution is wholly inconceivable. The same applies to raw materials. Our only hope of securing justice in distribution, proper appreciation abroad of the effort we made to assist foreign nations, and proper return for the service that we will perform revolve around complete independence of commitment to joint action on our part."

ous to any interested observer. "Real conflicts over policy will certainly arise, perhaps especially between the United Kingdom and North America." [20] The U.S.S.R. has played a great role in the war and will certainly be a powerful agent in the peace. China has been in the front line against aggression longer than any other nation. A united front among the United Nations when conflicting policies and even conflicting ideologies emerge in the peace negotiations cannot be taken for granted.

This fact alone makes imperative the creation of collaborative machinery, the working out of principles and policies, and even the negotiation of commitments that can be brought into action when the time for reconstruction arrives. This is not to suggest the driving of bargains, but rather the devising of machinery for joint deliberation and decision on problems that will certainly not be easy to solve. Such machinery has already been created and works smoothly in the various organs of United States–Canadian collaboration. Difficult as the extension of such procedures may be, the effort would seem worth making in view of the dangers to be confronted in the short run and the purposes to be achieved in the long run.

[20] *Ibid.*, p. 37. *Cf. also* Geoffrey Crowther, "Anglo-American Pitfalls," *Foreign Affairs* (October, 1941).

CHAPTER III

THE POLITICAL BASIS
OF ECONOMIC
CO-OPERATION

The Power of the United Nations

THE POLITICAL conditions essential for the establishment of workable economic co-operation are simply stated. Any arrangement which gives reasonable assurance of durable peace, of security from aggression, and therefore of relief from crushing armament expenditures, will also enable long-term investment to be undertaken, specialization and interdependence to be risked, and trade barriers to be reduced. No consideration of plans for international economic co-operation can omit the statement that:

"Fundamentally, international economic and financial problems depend for their solution upon the preservation of peace and the restoration of political confidence and security." [1]

[1] Carnegie Endowment for International Peace, "Recommendations of the International Conference" (held at Chatham House, London, March 5–7, 1935).

It is, however, easier to state this elementary fact than to suggest ways and means by which peace may be restored and maintained. This agenda does not pretend to offer a blueprint for peace. The legal, political, and strategic aspects of a possible postwar world are here touched upon only in so far as they impinge upon economic reorganization. The multitude of thorny problems relating to boundaries, colonies, guarantees of peace and their sanctions, procedures for the pacific settlement of disputes, the development, interpretation, and enforcement of international law, the creation of international legal and political institutions, their powers and functions *vis-à-vis* their member-states and the individual citizens of those states, and the choice between regional and universal organization are considerations that lie outside the scope of economic discussion. It is in this field of political reorganization that most of the unknowns in the equation of the future lie.

While no project of economic reorganization can have living reality until these unknowns are determined, certain assumptions can tentatively be made and certain questions may at least be raised. The assumptions made below are based on the eight points of the Atlantic Charter, supplemented by official statements of leading democratic statesmen as to the kind of postwar organization for which plans will be, and perhaps are being, made. The eight points included in the joint declaration of the President of the United

States and the Prime Minister of Great Britain run as follows: [2]

"First, their countries seek no aggrandizement, territorial or other;

"Second, they desire to see no territorial changes that do not accord with the freely expressed wishes of the peoples concerned;

"Third, they respect the right of all peoples to choose the form of government under which they will live; and they wish to see sovereign rights and self-government restored to those who have been forcibly deprived of them;

"Fourth, they will endeavor, with due respect for their existing obligations, to further the enjoyment by all States, great or small, victor or vanquished, of access, on equal terms, to the trade and to the raw materials of the world which are needed for their economic prosperity;

"Fifth, they desire to bring about the fullest collaboration between all nations in the economic field with the object of securing, for all, improved labor standards, economic advancement, and social security;

"Sixth, after the final destruction of the Nazi tyranny, they hope to see established a peace which will afford to all nations the means of dwelling in safety within their own boundaries, and which will afford assurance that all the men in all the lands may

[2] Department of State, *Bulletin* (August 16, 1941), Vol. V, No. 112, Publication 1632, pp. 125–26.

live out their lives in freedom from fear and want;

"SEVENTH, such a peace should enable all men to traverse the high seas and oceans without hindrance;

"EIGHTH, they believe that all of the nations of the world, for realistic as well as spiritual reasons, must come to the abandonment of the use of force. Since no future peace can be maintained if land, sea, or air armaments continue to be employed by nations which threaten, or may threaten, aggression outside of their frontiers, they believe, pending the establishment of a wider and permanent system of general security, that the disarmament of such nations is essential. They will likewise aid and encourage all other practicable measures which will lighten for peace-loving peoples the crushing burden of armaments."

Even if Mr. Churchill, on his return to London after the Atlantic meeting, had not bluntly interpreted the eighth point of the Charter as meaning the disarmament of Germany (and presumably its allies) until more permanent means of collective security can be devised, many other responsible pronouncements would have left no doubt that the democratic powers intend to administer and control the transitional arrangements of the postwar world. They will make a politically hard but economically generous peace.

This would seem to involve acceptance of responsibility for the maintenance of order, the restoration of effective government in areas now under the control of aggressor nations, the reprovisioning of devastated regions, and supervision if not occupation of the beaten enemy countries. While commitments as to boundaries have been wisely avoided, the first three points of the Charter would seem to indicate that forceful partition or dismemberment of the enemy countries is not contemplated. The fifth point of the Charter and other statements, notably the address by President Roosevelt at the closing session of the International Labor Conference on November 6, 1941, clearly contemplate international organization particularly for the achievement of economic and social aims.

There has been a marked silence, however, in regard to any proposals for the reorganization of international institutions in the political sphere, and what appears to be a studied avoidance of such phrases as "collective security." It seems reasonable to assume that, at least during the immediate postwar period, reliance will not be placed upon treaty formulas or international institutions. Effective power will be exercised directly by the victorious United Nations. Their opponents will be disarmed and kept disarmed, and no commitment has been made in the meantime as to the method by which order will be kept after the transitional period.

The democratic countries evidently intend, therefore, to keep in their own hands effective power to reorganize the postwar world and determine what political machinery, if any, can ultimately be devised for the preservation of peace. There have been two broad trends of thought and action in this respect which are of direct significance for a consideration of postwar economic problems. The first of these trends is toward limitation of national sovereignty; the next three sections of this chapter are concerned mainly with this problem. The second trend is toward universal co-operation in the economic field. This is treated specifically in the last section, though it is, in a sense, the subject of the entire chapter.

Regionalism in Europe

There has, until recently, been much discussion of regionalism. This appears in part to have been a re-action from the disillusion that resulted in Europe from the failure to achieve any effective means of collective security in the prewar period. There has been wide-spread belief in responsible quarters that the problem of security demands precise commitments that are obtainable only on a regional basis. The growing discussion of federal ideas, particularly in Europe, has also been a factor.[3] So has the movement toward reliance

[3] *Cf.*, e. g., "Blueprint for a Post-War World," Interview with Julian Huxley, *New York Times Magazine* (January 28, 1940): "A League system will not work because it is a contradiction in terms: the absolute sovereignty of its member-states is irreconcilable with collective action for the benefit of the whole. Some abrogation of sovereignty—in other words a step towards federation—is essential."

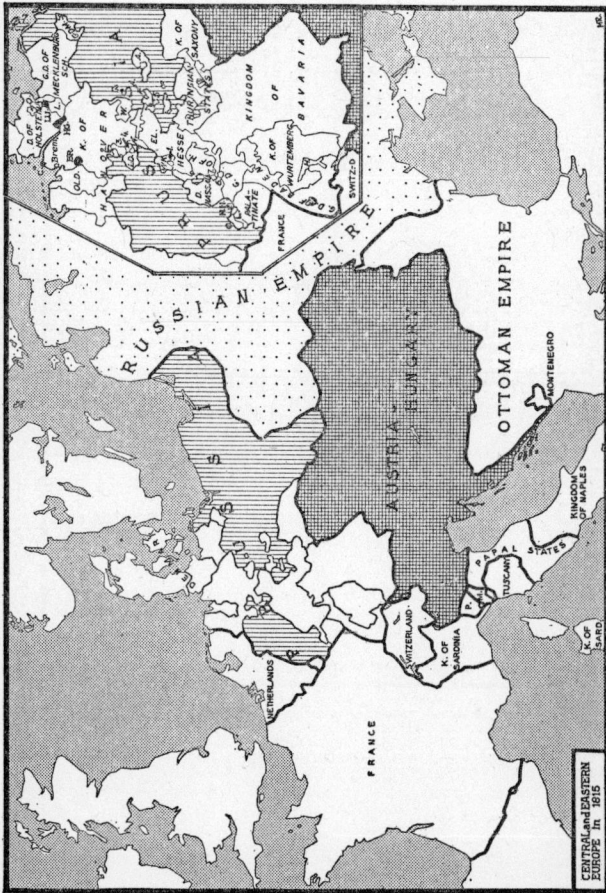

FIGURE 1

D. Duchy, G.D. Grand Duchy, EL. Electorate, K. Kingdom; BR. Bremen, Brem. Bremerhaven, C. Cuxhaven, HG. Hamburg, LU. Lubeck; A. Duchy of Anhalt, G.D. of H. Grand Duchy of Hesse, G.D.M.S. Grand Duchy of Mecklenburg Strelitz, H. Principality of Hohenzollern, H.H. Hesse-Homburg, L. Principality of Lichtenberg, L.D. Lippe-Detmold, M. Modena, O. to Oldenburg, OLD. Oldenburg, P. Parma, SCH. Schwerin, W. Duchy of Brunswick, WK. Principality of Waldeck; 1 to G.D. of Hesse, 2 Schaumburg-Lippe, 3 Electoral Hesse, 4 Pyrmont To P. of Waldeck, 5 to Kingdom of Hanover, 6 Frankfort, 7 Homburg to Lippe-Detmold.

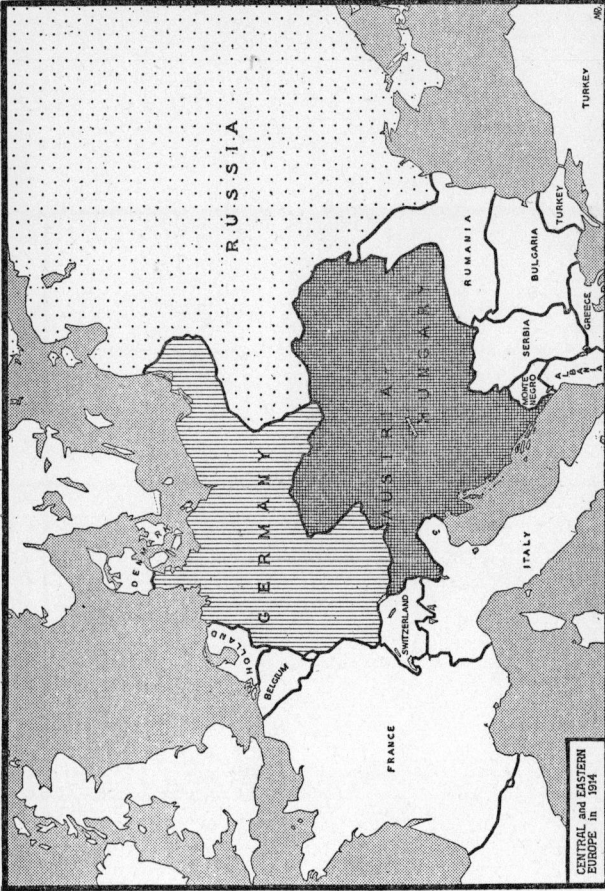

CENTRAL and EASTERN EUROPE in 1914

FIGURE 2

on a more even balance of power in Europe rather than a United States of Europe. Thus, in the closing days of the International Labor Conference held at New York in November, 1941, an official statement by the exiled governments of Czechoslovakia, Greece, Poland, and Yugoslavia announced an agreement to create a central European bloc which, it was hoped, might later include Austria, Hungary, Roumania, and possibly Bulgaria.[4]

It may perhaps be doubted how far this rather sudden proposal has popular support in the countries concerned. Whether it can be carried effectively to the point of political federation cannot be estimated. Whether other similar arrangements can be made, for example, among the Scandinavian countries, so that Germany will face two or three approximately equal powers on the Continent, is equally impossible to forecast. If such a development should take place, it would create an entirely different situation, politically and economically, in Europe. After the last war the victorious Allies, applying the principle of self-determination, divided the peoples of central and eastern Europe into independent sovereign states. They failed to cooperate, and it was not long before a reinvigorated Germany conquered them.

Even if ambitious political attempts to form regional

[4] *New York Times* (November 4, 1941), p. 8; *also* (November 3, 1941), p. 3.

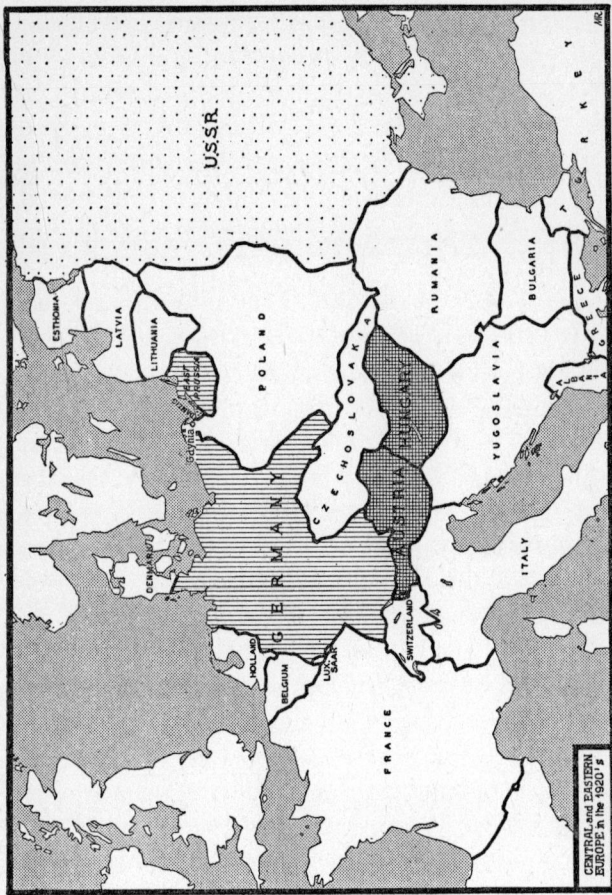

CENTRAL and EASTERN
EUROPE in the 1920's

FIGURE 3

groups should fall short of achievement, it would seem
probable that for the purposes of economic collaboration there will be a reaction in some form from the
prewar situation of unfettered national sovereignty
exercised over small areas. Such sovereignty was in fact
largely an illusion, since independent action by small
states has narrow limits; but it was nonetheless destructive in the sphere of international economic co-
operation.

The difficulties of the regional idea, however,
quickly become evident even in Europe. The economic
interests of the Scandinavian countries, for example,
are closely bound up with the markets offered for
their production and shipping by the great trading
powers. Norwegian shipping, whaling, and fishing;
Swedish mechanical, timber, paper, and pulp industries; Danish dairying; and Finnish forestry are dependent upon the world market. These countries have developed close political and cultural relations among
themselves, but their economic organization is directed
toward the outside world rather than to regional trade.
It is sometimes suggested that Switzerland, Belgium,
and Holland, which in times past were parties to the
so-called Oslo discussions, might form part of a north-
ern federation; but the political, cultural, and economic
interests of Belgium and Holland are bound up with
their colonial empires and their trade with Britain and
the United States. Switzerland is *sui generis,* and might
find the best solution of its problems in the continuance

of permanent neutrality as the center of international
institutions.

Regionalism in the Far East

Outside Europe, the difficulties of finding even approximately integrated regional areas offering some
practical possibility of effective organization are still
more obvious. The Far East, which is often glibly referred to in this connection, may be taken as an example.[5] If India is included, the Far Eastern countries
muster approximately half the world's population, but
it is a population with staggering economic problems
likely to be aggravated by new trends of population
increase, and with a political and social background
vastly different from that of the Western World. Any
attempt to group this area in a regional federation
would present even a weakened Japan with opportunities paralleled only by those which a United States
of Europe would offer to a reviving Germany. The
withdrawal of British and American influence from
southeast Asia would create a vacuum into which
Japan would irresistibly be drawn, as recent events in
Indo-China have demonstrated. Moreover the British
Dominions in the Pacific, to say nothing of the Euro-

[5] The paragraphs which follow are based on an unpublished
manuscript by Mr. W. L. Holland, prepared for the International
Secretariat of the Institute of Pacific Relations.

pean colonial powers, have a vital interest in the security and economic development of this area.

An ingenious plan for the creation of regional institutions in the Far East has been suggested in default of the restoration of freer world trade and effective means of ensuring collective security on a world scale.[6] It proceeds in stages. The first involves the creation in southeast Asia of an Indonesian federation or bloc, consisting of the Philippines, Burma, the Netherlands Indies, and British Malaya, to which Indo-China and Thailand might later be added. This federation might be brought into existence and guaranteed by a consolidation of military force based on Singapore, Hong Kong, Batavia, and Manila. So protected and guaranteed, Indonesia might proceed to develop joint technical and economic services looking toward the promotion of an international reconstruction project. Such a plan would be conceived as modernization under the tutelage of the United States, France, the Netherlands, and the British Commonwealth.

This hypothetical regional organization in the Far East, projected upon the measures of military, political, and economic collaboration now being developed in the course of the Pacific war, is in itself a difficult and complex proposal. It would obviously encounter obstacles arising from the nascent nationalism of the peoples involved, as well as from commercial rivalries among the great powers. But if its achievement should

[6] *Ibid.*

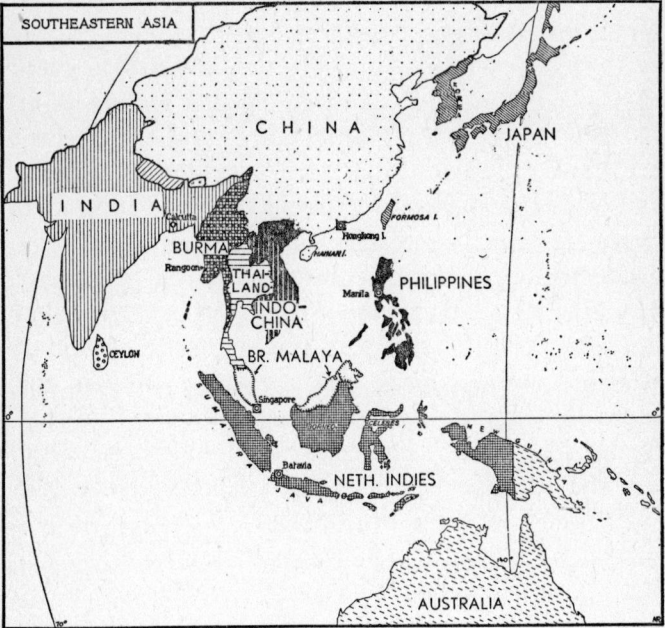

FIGURE 4

prove possible it would merely consolidate the colonial and semicolonial areas of southeast Asia. Great as such an achievement would be, it is far from the formation of a Far Eastern region. There would still be, as in Europe if the central European bloc takes practical form, a balance-of-power problem. Not only Indonesia, but China, Japan, the U.S.S.R., and India would be the units to reckon with. The influence of the United States, Britain, the Netherlands, and France would presumably be exerted largely through Indonesia, a fact which in itself would make Indonesia an arena for international rivalries. Even this complication omits the obvious difficulty that the trading powers with no colonies in this region, including Germany, Italy, and Japan, would be vitally interested in any scheme of international reorganization affecting these rich raw-material areas.

Moreover, it seems clear that no effective balance of power could be maintained in the Far East merely by attempting to organize a regional pact or a network of bilateral pacts between India, Indonesia, China, Japan, and the U.S.S.R. The promotion of improved political relations and more effective technical and economic relations between these countries is a task worthy of effort; but ultimately the peace of the Pacific must be assured, if at all, by some such means as an expansion and strengthening of the Nine-Power Pact to guarantee, and to provide effective machinery for guaranteeing, the territorial integrity, not of China alone but

of all the Pacific countries. Not only the original signa-
tories, but the British Pacific Dominions and the
U.S.S.R. would need to be parties to such a pact. Like
the original Nine Power Pact, it would be without any
but moral force unless it provided machinery for enforcement and also for handling disputes and for promoting agreements in regard to such matters as armaments, fortifications, air traffic, fisheries, and migration.
It would involve practically all the major world powers
and bear directly upon their policies in other areas. At
this point it becomes clear that what is involved is de-
centralized organization of something equivalent to a
world-wide League of Nations, or a world system of
balanced power.

The Limits of Regionalism

Any realistic analysis of regional proposals invaria-
bly leads back to this point. This is in some measure because the regional idea is tainted with the continental-
ism of *Geopolitik*. Professor Staley has pointed out in
a recent article that continental neighborhood is in
many cases merely a cartographic illusion.[7] The ties
that bind people together are common cultural, economic, and strategic interests; and these do not depend
wholly by any means upon continental proximity. In-

[7] Eugene Staley, "The Myth of the Continents," *Foreign Affairs*
(April, 1941).

deed, the way maps are necessarily drawn has deluded some not very profound students into forgetting that distance is not merely a matter of miles, but also of time and cost; that not only the land, but the sea and the air also are important means of communication. What is even more naïve is the mistake, so well pointed out by Staley, that distances which ought to be measured on a globe are often confused by the distortion of areas on the more familiar projections used in most school atlases.

It is true that grave political and strategic problems often arise between continental peoples cooped up in narrow abutting areas. Particularly in Europe, regional security pacts and a more even balance of power are probably needed; but they should be negotiated within an assured system of international order. On the economic side, it is impossible to carve out limited areas of regional self-sufficiency. Attempts to do so canalize trade into uneconomic bilateralism and bolster up inefficient vested interests in the areas so organized. Moreover, in a rapidly changing world, many little countries have shown a better sense of economic realities, more flexibility, and greater powers of adaptation than large economic units, especially where the latter are built upon a nice balance of conflicting sectional interests.

The great strides recently taken toward regional understanding in the Western Hemisphere do not contradict but support the views expressed above. Real progress has been made because there has been a realistic appreciation of the limits within which regionalism is a desirable policy. The American republics do not form an economic bloc and do not aim at regional self-sufficiency. The essence of the good-neighbor policy is not preferential or exclusive. The mutual economic and cultural interests of the Americas are developing rapidly; but not at the expense, or to the exclusion, of other powers. The trade agreements that have been negotiated contain most-favored-nation clauses and are aimed at the extension of multilateral trade based upon equality of trading opportunity. In the political sphere, understanding and co-operation have been promoted not as a form of security against aggressive action within the group, but because the good-neighbor policy disavows such action. The friendly republics of the Americas are good neighbors because, and to the degree in which, they are good citizens of the world community.

There is, therefore, no escape by way of regional organization from the ultimate political problem of ensuring peace in the world by some effective universal force. Regional organization within a universal pattern may usefully cope with specific localized issues; but ultimately peace depends either upon effective power being exercized by some dominant group, or upon some organized system of collective security, or upon approximately equal forces being neutralized in some balance of power. Almost any organization in which the United States is an active partner will have great influence. The extraordinary development of air power has completely upset former conceptions of security, whether regional or collective. It has rendered isolation and neutrality illusory, especially for small peoples. On the other hand, it might offer an effective instrument of police power if the political problems of collective security could be solved.

For the transitional period when this war ends, it would seem that the choice has been made. The United Nations intend, when they win, to maintain in their own hands the dominant force—air power, sea power, and industrial potential—upon which peace will rest. There will be few to quarrel with this realistic decision for the interim period. Not many students of international affairs retain any illusions about the possibility of maintaining peace and promoting co-operation without effective power to enforce them. But Holy Alliances do not have a long life. The only ultimate justification for an interim hegemony by the United Nations must be the use of that hegemony to establish some wider and more effective mechanism for the maintenance of peace, either by a new and more realistic system of collective security or by the creation of new states to secure regional balances of power within a wider system of balanced power.

Since the entry of the United States into the war, discussion of regional federations or blocs has diminished. This is for the simple reason that a universal organization of world order can be envisaged if, and only if, the United States is an active member. Since the United States entered the war, there has been more discussion again of international institutions and of limitations of national sovereignty in a collective system. One fact is very clear. The small countries are ready to accept any limitation and any commitment which the United States will accept.

International Economic Co-operation

The second trend referred to above is that toward universal co-operation in the economic field. There is accumulating evidence that international machinery is contemplated for the achievement of technical, economic, and social, as distinct from political, collaboration. If no other evidence were available, the maintenance in being and operation of the League's technical services (in particular, economic research, opium and health), of the International Labor Organization, and of the Bank for International Settlements would suggest such a policy.

The International Labor Organization, of which the United States is a member, in November, 1941, held a regular conference in New York attended by representatives of thirty-two nation-states, with far-reaching discussion of plans for economic and social reconstruction. Its meeting was chosen as the vehicle for

announcement of the projected central European bloc.
It was opened by an address from the Secretary of
Labor and closed by a speech from the President of
the United States at a special session held in the White
House. Its agenda was concerned primarily with projects for postwar policies based upon social welfare,
and co-ordinated internationally in an attempt to
achieve planned international equilibrium in pursuance
of the fifth point of the Atlantic Charter.

The use of international machinery is indeed implicit in the wording of this point, which reads: "They
desire to bring about the fullest collaboration between
all nations in the economic field, with the object of
securing, for all, improved labor standards, economic
advancement and social security." It is not so implicit
in the fourth point, which merely states that "they
will endeavor, with due respect for their existing obligations, to further the enjoyment by all states, great
or small, victor or vanquished, of access, on equal
terms, to the trade and to the raw materials of the
world which are needed for their economic prosperity."

These statements, supported by the drift of economic discussion of these matters in the democratic
countries, leave no doubt that an effort will be made
to plan national and international economic policies
in the postwar world so that international relations may
be built upon expanding national prosperity. This ob-

jective, often stated elliptically in the phrase "social security," involves some measure of national economic planning and some machinery for the international co-ordination of national plans as well as some measure of planning and action by supranational agencies. The chapters which follow are postulated upon acceptance of this objective as a realistic assumption based on present policies and commitments.

The three assumptions stated in this chapter may, therefore, be summarized as, first, the recognition by the United Nations of their responsibility in the transition period for the maintenance of international order and the control of international collaboration; second, an effort to limit the exercise of sovereignty by independent nation-states; and, third, commitment to policies of social welfare involving the international co-ordination of national economic policies and the creation of supranational institutions.

These assumptions leave aside the ultimate political problems of peace and international machinery for its preservation. They are realistic assumptions in the sense that they represent the political bases upon which, after an Allied victory, economic reconstruction will probably be attempted. In the long run, however, the overriding problem of peace will reassert itself. No group of nations, however powerful, can for long maintain a peace of domination; the limitation of national sovereignty demands the creation of effective supranational (not merely international) institutions; and social welfare demands for its achievement the integrated co-operation and action through common agencies that is the positive aspect of assured peace.

CHAPTER IV

THE MEANING OF
SOCIAL SECURITY

Insecurity of Restrictive Nationalism

EVERY important pronouncement regarding peace aims is now built upon some sweeping, but usually vague, statement about social security, social welfare, or social justice.[1]

A cynic might ascribe this promise of a brave new world to a lively realization of the social and political dangers that accompanied the violent economic fluctuations and prolonged unemployment caused by the last war and its ensuing crises. There is an obvious desire at all costs to forestall repetition of these troubles.

The demand for an increased measure of social security, however, has far deeper roots. It is not merely a bribe in advance to future veterans. Behind it lies a vivid memory of the failure to achieve economic adjustment and stability between 1918 and 1939. The

[1] *Cf.*, e. g., the fifth point of the Atlantic statement: "They desire to bring about the fullest collaboration between all nations in the economic field, with the object of securing, for all, improved labor standards, economic advancement and social security."

nineteenth-century system of cosmopolitan capitalist enterprise could not be satisfactorily restored after the war of 1914–18 because the conditions necessary for its functioning were not present. There was no assurance of peace, and therefore no political stability on which to build international economic co-operation.

Moreover, a vast and complex series of economic maladjustments and disequilibria had developed within each country and between them. Each national economic system had developed independently. The structure of costs and prices in each had been adjusted to the production of war materials. The machine industries, for example, had been greatly expanded in practically every country. Some wage rates had risen above the general level. The cost of living and wage rates in general were equated to high levels of commodity prices. When commodity prices fell abruptly in the first postwar crisis there was heavy pressure on the wage rates and much unemployment.

Adjustments of costs, and particularly wages, to the new levels of prices that would have been set by free competition, were necessary. These adjustments involved social and political difficulties that proved in many cases to be too great for governments to face. Agricultural production in Europe could not cope with the expanded and mechanized low-cost production in the United States and other overseas countries. New manufacturing industries were faced by competition from older industrial areas. Workers released from armament industries or demobilized from the armies flooded the labor market.

After the first postwar crisis and the inflationary upheavals in central Europe had brought some measure of effective, if harsh, liquidation in most countries, an attempt was made to restore international equilibrium. This attempt took the form of restoring the international gold standard by a series of national monetary stabilizations. The levels at which successive countries went back to the gold standard were unilaterally determined, so that exchange disequilibria added to the maladjustments of prices. This aggravation occurred particularly in the case of the British return to prewar parity in 1925 and the French stabilization at an unduly low level in 1927 and 1928. For a few years, from 1925 to 1929, the instability of the exchanges was masked by a great and continuing flow of loans, primarily from the United States to Europe. The loan flow papered over the cracks and for a time made it possible to expand international trade without much change in the national patterns of production; but even in these years there were steadily rising tariffs designed to safeguard national industries from the pressure of external competition. In 1929, the credit inflation in the United States collapsed and within two years the international gold standard had collapsed with it. Its restoration had been a futile gesture, since the necessary conditions for its successful operation could not be restored.[2]

There is now little dissent from the view that

"a great part of the practical opposition expressed in recent years to freer trading initiatives and to exchange stabilization springs from such motives of social welfare as concern with national or group standards of living, the distress arising from unemployment and the desire to mitigate, and if possible control, the violent cyclical fluctuations of economic activity that bring insecurity to employers as well as employed. It must be recognized that there is a widespread and powerful popular opinion that deems it intolerable for human beings to live in the shadow of economic insecurity, poverty, malnutrition and unemployment. Arguments for freer trade based upon laissez faire and the long-run maximizing of national income are often rejected because of the preoccupation with social security in the short run and the demand for safeguarding employment." [3]

Social security and employment were not in fact safeguarded after the last war by breaking up the world market into a series of protected national markets. Restrictive economic nationalism did not solve the problem, since it did not remove the causes of maladjustment in the national economic systems. Indeed, it aggravated the maladjustments that should have been cured. In 1939, it could be said that

[2] Cf. J. B. Condliffe, *The Reconstruction of World Trade* (New York, 1940), chs. 1–3.

[3] *The Changing Structure of Economic Life*, International Chamber of Commerce, Document No. 1 (Copenhagen, 1939).

"the tragedy of most government intervention in recent years is that it has been negative, a series of efforts to buttress and preserve this or that group interest. Necessarily such intervention becomes more and more restrictive and in so doing defeats its own purposes. It imposes rigidity where there should be adaptability, maintains prices that should fall, reduces production in low-cost areas and fosters it where costs are high." [4]

The fact is that the restrictions which went so far to destroy international economic co-operation in the years between the wars were not undertaken in defense of the underprivileged but in protection of the over-privileged and inefficient. Not unemployment and wages so much as property values were buttressed by price and production controls, quotas and tariff protection. Social security is not incompatible with international equilibrium, but the protection of inefficient industries against external competition is. The countries which have the longest experience and fullest development of social-security legislation, such as Great Britain, the Scandinavian countries, Australia, and New Zealand, have not found it incompatible with a high level of international trade.

The Need for Adaptation

This experience of the last postwar period, still imperfectly understood, is very relevant to the problems

[4] *Ibid.*

that will certainly present themselves at the close of the present war. Once again there will surely be profound maladjustments and disequilibria, both national and international. It should be emphasized that the correction of those maladjustments will be a painful but necessary process. If peace and prosperity are to be restored, men must be taken from war industries to peace production, trade must flow again, prices must be brought into competitive equilibrium, and costs must be adjusted. Some wages must come down because the marginal efficiency of certain types of labor will be reduced; some property values must be written off. If the transition is to be made as quickly and as easily as possible, these changes must be made so as to promote rather than hinder mobility of labor and capital.

It is highly improbable, however, that any country will find it politically possible, or socially desirable, to allow free international competition to bring about the necessary transfer of labor and capital from war to peace industries. This would mean throwing workers into wholesale unemployment, and inflicting heavy capital losses upon the war-stimulated industries. It would also mean wholesale wage reductions and drastic declines of commodity prices.

International equilibrium must be restored. There must be national adjustments to the new equilibrium brought about in large measure by competitive forces. But it is unlikely that a world market can be suddenly restored, into which national economies must be trimmed by the ruthless pressure of competition, entailing heavy sacrifices on those whose scanty economic resources do not give them adequate bargaining power.

Such a course cannot now be followed for two good reasons. No democratic electorate will refrain from demanding government intervention to mitigate the ruthlessness of unregulated competition. And there has been too recent experience of the manner in which such competition leads quickly to a downward spiral of deflation which is needlessly destructive, and in the long run ineffective to bring the desired adjustment. The lesson must be learned, however, that social security is not won by protecting vested interests. "Stability which leads to stagnation gives no security." [5] Effective security in a changing world comes through "masterful administration of the unforeseen."

Maintenance of Employment

If neither laissez faire nor restrictive economic nationalism can provide a solution for this problem, is there any practicable alternative? No one with any experience of international political realities is likely to give a dogmatically confident answer to such a ques-

[5] Bank for International Settlements, Eleventh Annual Report (June, 1941), p. 191.

tion; but at least a possible and even promising line of approach to the problem may be presented. That approach may be summarized as an attempt to utilize national monetary and fiscal policies to sustain employment while achieving progressive correction of price-cost maladjustments by laying emphasis upon the encouragement of new employment opportunities. An illustration may be sketched briefly. The new war industries in many areas of the United States have attracted labor to areas with inadequate housing. Families live in trailers or other makeshift accommodations. Housing development (including city improvements and slum clearance) is needed, and also improvement of transportation facilities, public services such as drainage, water supplies, electric mains, and educational equipment.

When the war ends some of the industries it has stimulated may well remain where they are. So will some of the workers, and for them at least the needs above listed must be satisfied. Others, however, must find work elsewhere—in new industries. Plans should be developed for public expenditure to build the schools, roads, bridges, and power plants that will be needed, both in areas of present production and in new areas that may be developed. Wage rates should be negotiated that will reduce the attractiveness of the overstimulated war industries and draw labor supply to the industries where development is both needed and possible. At the same time privileged monopolistic groups, whether of labor or capital, should not be allowed to hold up the development of new employment opportunities or to withhold opportunities of providing low-cost conveniences for consumers. Increased mobility of labor and capital is one of the keys to the whole situation.

At the end of hostilities it is reasonable to expect a considerable accumulation of demand for a great variety of consumers' goods whose supply has been curtailed during the war period. This accumulated demand, supplemented by foreign demands for foods and raw materials, may well cause a considerable revival of private enterprise and investment; but unless the government is prepared, when the first private demands slacken off, to embark upon public expenditures for the building of public equipment, such as schools, roads, and bridges, and to provide the necessary conditions for low-cost rehousing, the immediate postwar recovery may be short-lived. One essential element of such a program is the reduction of wartime expenditure and the maintenance of a tax program designed on the one hand to keep control of the postwar replacement boom and on the other to bring the national budget into balance during the boom.

National monetary and taxation programs, therefore, should be designed to restrain the first replacement boom within reasonable limits and to sustain national income, purchasing power, and employment when the boom shows signs of flagging. These programs should be aimed not at protecting industries that ought to decline, but at stimulating industries where expansion is possible. They should indeed aim at the same sort of balanced cost-price structure that would be brought about if competition were free to work. If they do not manage to achieve such a balance, they will aggravate the maladjustments and worsen unemployment in the long run.

This means that the tax program should encourage new investment in certain types of developing industries, that wage rates in some industries must come down, and that lower prices for surplus products must be allowed to discourage further production. It also means that government expenditures, launched to sustain employment when the first replacement boom slackens off, should be designed so as to stimulate rather than supplant private enterprise. Government action to replan cities and their approaches might well bring forth a great volume of private building enterprise. Public works along the lines of the Tennessee Valley Authority would promote investment and sustain employment in the strategic heavy industries.

From a realistic political standpoint there can be no doubt that the restoration of international co-operation must be correlated with national employment policies. It must proceed from the parts to the whole, as well as from the whole to the parts. The establishment of exchange stability and the freeing of international trade must be the result, even more than the means, of achieving national equilibrium. National economic policies are the center of interest. The main front of international action is the home front.[6] The reduction of price-cost disequilibria so that private enterprise can function again must be an essential element of national economic policies if they are to be successful. But it will be easier to achieve such results if national economic activity is maintained at a high level than if it goes first into an inflationary boom and then into a deflationary tailspin.

Essentials of Social Security

The editor of the London *Economist* has recently stated the dilemma of national economic policies in terms of failure to secure a balance instead of a mixture of freedom and order.[7] His statement is so directly relevant to this discussion that its main argument is reproduced here:

[6] This is consistent with historical experience. *Cf.*, e. g., Arnold J. Toynbee, *A Study of History*, Vol. III, p. 196: "This transference of the field of action, which we discern in Shakespeare's presentation of his heroes when we arrange these fictitious personalities in an ascending order of spiritual growth, can also be discerned in the histories of civilizations. Here too, when a series of responses to challenges accumulates into a growth, we shall find, as this growth proceeds, that the field of action is shifting, all the time, from the external environment of the growing society into the interior of the society's own body social."

[7] Geoffrey Crowther, "Where Do We Go from Here?" *Fortune* (October, 1941), p. 94.

"Reasons why a democratic electorate is unlikely to accept FREEDOM as the dominant principle of a democratic economy:

1. A regime of free private enterprise results in the existence of great masses of underprivileged persons. The state must intervene to assert the doctrine of humanitarianism.
2. An uncontrolled system has shown itself to be subject to swings of boom and slump far more violent than a democracy, in the twentieth century, can tolerate without interference.

Reasons why a democratic electorate is unlikely to accept ORDER as the dominant principle of a democratic economy:

1. No centrally controlled system, working through a vast bureaucracy, can be as efficient in the production of goods as a freely competitive system. The standard of living depends on productive efficiency.
2. There is a natural right for a man to follow his inventive genius and his enterprising spirit wherever they lead. A state in which the government controls all economic activity approaches the totalitarian. And the democratic election of the central government is an inadequate safeguard while there are fanatics, machine bosses, demagogues and adventurers."

In seeking a balance between the principles of free enterprise and social security in national economies, it is inevitable that those countries which have achieved revaluation of social purposes under the stress of war shall strive to preserve and consolidate the sense of national unity and cohesion. This goes far beyond the merely charitable aim of preventing or relieving distress. Social security in the old sense of the word is a part of national economic policy that is bound to be extended and strengthened. The "National Minimum," as it has come to be called in England, involves that

"the citizen of a democracy should be guaranteed as of right, enough food to maintain him in health. He should be assured of a minimum standard of shelter, clothing, and fuel. He should be given full and equal opportunities of education. He should have leisure and facilities for enjoying it. He should be secured against the risk of unemployment, ill-health, and old age. Above all, the presence of children should not be allowed to bring with it misery for the parents, deprivation for the children, and poverty for all. All these things inhere in the individual as his citizen's rights." [8]

Many similar statements might be cited from widely different sources to show how the concept of social security has been extended. An analysis of the concept by an American expert committee covers a wide field, even though it is confined to a consideration of social security for the wage earner: security for employment (education, employment offices, resettlement, and soil-conservation programs); security in the availability of employment; security in employment; security of income while employed; security of reasonable standards of working conditions; security of some income while unemployed; security of retirement income; of recreation; of self-improvement and self-development; of

[8] *Ibid.*

medical and hospital assistance; security of one's family in case of one's accident, invalidity, ill-health, or death.[9]

It seems clear that the so-called social services, pensions, unemployment insurance, medical care, as well as trade-union organization and factory legislation have received impetus as a result of the war.[10] But the demand for social reorganization goes much further than these can carry. It is, in essence, a demand that in a large area of co-operative economic activity the profit motive actuating private enterprise shall be replaced by the incentive of social service, including community duties in counterpart of citizen's rights. In this area the social incentive is destined to "become dominant, and if private business remains in this sector (as it undoubtedly will) it must expect to conform to the promptings of that incentive." [11] The area includes the provision of public services, such as education, water, sanitation, and, in the more developed democratic countries, transport, communication, and electrical power.

These are long steps toward the socialization of public-utility services, and the effective scope of such common action is clearly debatable from country to country. Moreover, there is some danger of forgetting

[9] Smith Simpson, *Draft Report of the Social Security Committee* (mimeographed). Commission to Study the Organization of Peace (New York, 1941).

[10] *Cf.* plan proposed for the United States by a group of economists, *New York Times* (January 2, 1942).

[11] Geoffrey Crowther, *op. cit.*

that the possibility of individual advancement in a progressive economy is a real factor in social contentment and a strong incentive to social progress. Economic opportunity has been one of the driving forces of the new democratic world, and it should not be overlain by too much concern for security if by security is meant protection of economic status.

A word should be said at this point concerning the harsh impact of violent social changes upon independent small producers and clerical workers, the little men and the white-collar men who are not protected by powerful unions and have little power to protect themselves. They are the forgotten men, suffering from rising costs of production and costs of living as prices go up, omitted from great schemes of government expenditure, skimped in priorities and rationing, and left to their own resources in depression. Their ranks are always swollen in the period of demobilization after a great war by the release to civilian life of large numbers of army specialists and officers. If the problem of social security is envisaged as a compact between the government, large-scale industry, and organized labor, then this large, independent, and enterprising body of organizers and technicians suffers heavily. The Fascist and National Socialist revolutions in Europe capitalized upon their frustration and despair after the last war. Similar movements may come again unless there is room for private enterprise and energy in an expanding economic system.

Co-ordination of Credit Policies

From the viewpoint of international economic co-operation, the most difficult and important extension of national economic policy lies in the field of credit control and manipulation designed to prevent or mitigate the unemployment resulting from violent fluctuations of prices and production. There is no doubt that national monetary policies will be governed largely by the desire to forestall unemployment. The projection of such policies is a fact. The possibility or desirability of realizing them is not at issue here. There will be much disagreement and debate on both counts. This is the essence of democratic government. But whether it is desirable or not, in a given country, to nationalize railroads or telephones, to embark upon great schemes or rehousing and slum clearance, or to devise methods of improved food distribution is not relevant to the present argument.

What seems definite is that, in the immediate post-war period, an effort will be made to promote public action over a wide field, not only to avert unemployment but also to achieve a greater measure of social welfare. The timing of effective plans for government action in such fields as state-aided housing, public health, education and nutrition, public-works programs, and an extension of social services is an important factor. Both adaptation to the new peacetime conditions and the creation of new employment opportunities are needed. It is as vital to prevent inflation and discourage the perpetuation of inefficient or extravagant production as it is to forestall deflationary spirals of unemployment. Flexibility and mobility in the industrial system are more effective means of security than resistance to change and attempts to protect the present pattern of employment.

CHAPTER V

THE DISPOSAL OF AGRICULTURAL SURPLUSES[1]

A Continuing Crisis

SOCIAL security is usually discussed in terms of the needs and risks of industrial urban workers. As great cities and large-scale industries developed in the nineteenth century, the workers massed in them became cogs in a great economic machine. Their work represented only specialized fractions of the total product, and the conditions of its organization passed completely out of their control. Moreover, they were cut off from the means of satisfying directly their needs for food, clothing, and shelter. They became utterly dependent upon the smooth functioning of specialized trade. If price relationships fell out of equilibrium so that profitable production diminished in their sector of industry, they were thrown into unemployment without the possibil-

[1] The author's thanks are due to the *Journal of Farm Economics* for permission to use the text of this chapter which was published as an article in the May, 1942, issue of that journal.

ity of providing for their needs in any other way than by wage labor. It is natural that from the cities came demands for the right to organize, for legislation to regulate hours and working conditions, for the provision of holidays, as well as the later movements to provide pensions, medical care, housing, unemployment insurance, and improved nutrition. In many countries, indeed, the opposition to such schemes has come from a combination of the wealthier sections of the urban population with the mass of country dwellers. Only in those countries where agriculture itself has taken long strides toward mechanization and "factories in the fields" has the extension of social services to rural labor been a vital issue.

Yet there is a very real sense in which social security for the farmer has been a prime object of recent protective legislation. There can be no doubt that a continuing agricultural crisis against which national governments strove desperately to protect their farming communities was one of the root causes of international economic disequilibrium in the period between the wars. The accumulating disequilibrium in the years 1923–1932 and again from 1936 onward is dramatically summarized in the table and diagram on pages 104–5.

This mounting index of agricultural surpluses and declining index of agricultural prices, even in the years of apparent prosperity and stability from 1925 to 1929, are eloquent evidence of underlying structural disequilibria in the world's agricultural production and con-

INDEX

300

250

200

150

100

50

0

STOCKS
PRICES

YEARS   1923 1924 1925 1926 1927 1928 1929 1930 1931 1932 1933 1934 1935 1936 1937 1938 1939

FIGURE 5

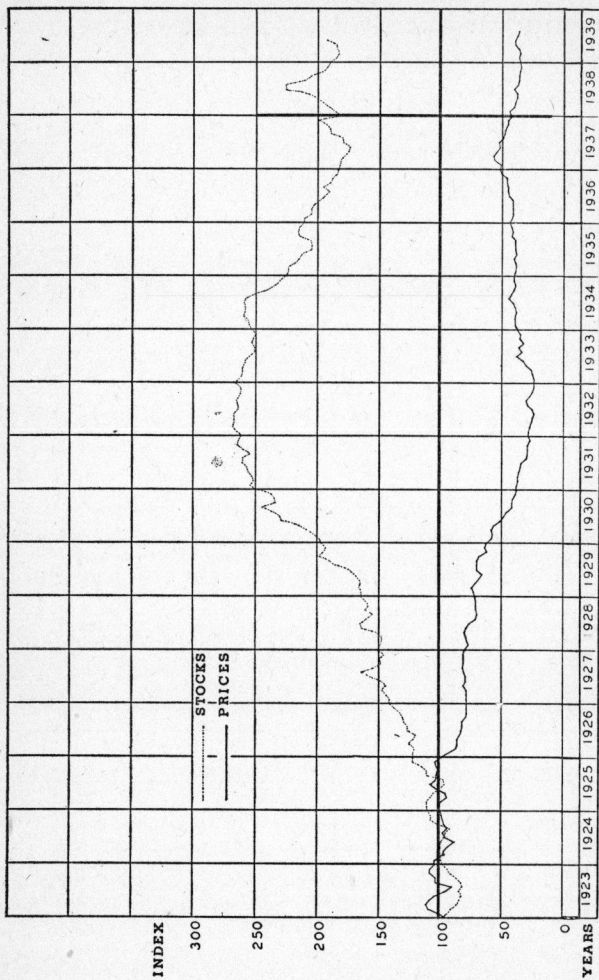

Composite indices of stocks and prices of principal agricultural commodities,
1923–1939

Composite Indices of Stocks and Prices of Principal Agricultural Commodities, 1923–1938 *

(*Average 1923–1925 = 100*)

DECEMBER	STOCKS	PRICES
1923	93[a]	107
1924	107	98[b]
1925	122	103
1926	138	78
1927	146	81
1928	161	71
1929	193	64
1930	238	39
1931	263	27
1932	262	24
1933	250	35
1934	231	40
1935	215	42
1936	184	50
1937	199	45
1938	192[c]	34

* The commodities chosen and weights used in compiling the indices are cotton (9), wheat (6), sugar (6), rubber (3), silk (2), coffee (2) and tea (1). Price data for 1923–1926 supplied directly by the Bureau of Foreign and Domestic Commerce, other prices and stocks from the Survey of Current Business.

a Rubber stocks not available.
b Wheat prices not available for February, 1924.
c Coffee prices and stocks not available after 1937.

sumption. The figures lend strong support to the view that

"the causes of the world economic crisis and the depression were not largely—and certainly not exclusively— monetary factors. For this reason, issue from the depression cannot be found in monetary measures alone. The adjustment of supply to demand in many lines is of primary importance." [2]

They indicate also that the measures of agricultural protection and relief undertaken by almost every government, so far from solving, accentuated the underlying disequilibrium. The story is a simple one. Surplus stocks accumulated in many overseas agricultural countries while their European markets were shut off during the war years 1914–18, but were rapidly liquidated in the immediate postwar boom. They were not nearly so large as the surpluses that accumulated later on. The Economic Committee of the League of Nations in 1935 recalled

"how the war, by taking millions of workers from the fields in the belligerent countries just when the armies were demanding more and more foodstuffs, gave an impetus to oversea agricultural production—particularly cereals—the effect of which is still apparent today.[3]

"For several years indeed after the close of hostilities,

[2] V. P. Timoshenko, *World Agriculture and the Depression* (Ann Arbor, 1933), p. 3.

[3] It may be noted that production was in any case increasing rapidly because of the introduction of machine methods utilizing new forms of motive power and the application of biological discoveries. The war demands accelerated this trend.

Europe continued to import considerable quantities of agricultural products—particularly cereals and meat—her return to her former productive capacity having been retarded by a series of concomitant causes, such as the Russian revolution and numerous agrarian reforms.

"But directly her producing capacity was again restored, about 1925, the balance between supply and demand was broken; prices were already on the downgrade, and the full force of the collapse was felt from 1930 onwards.

"Exporting countries with a surplus of goods had to bear the full shock of this catastrophe against which they possessed only one means of defense—a useful means at first, but one which was later to constitute an additional danger—namely to slow down the marketing of their crops by accumulating stocks.

"On the other hand, agricultural producers in the importing countries with a shortage of crops were obliged to appeal to their Governments and to national solidarity in order to escape the contagion. This means they have used, and abused: the introduction of duties two or three times higher than world prices, ever stricter rationing, the reduction to close upon vanishing-point of the proportion of foreign products admitted in the various preparations, bounties for production, export bounties, 'schemes,' monopolies and other forms of planned economy.[4]

"These Draconian measures, which, quite apart from the disorder which they caused in the delicate and complex mechanism of the balance of international accounts,

---

[4] The essential reason for these developments was the breakdown of trading and exchange equilibrium, in which United States tariffs played a not unimportant role. *Cf.* J. B. Condliffe, *The Reconstruction of World Trade*, ch. 5.

tend to create as many different price regimes as there
are protectionist countries and thus delay a return to
the essential system of non-watertight compartments,
were followed by a whole series of difficulties. . . . This
situation, taken as a whole, represents a defensive reaction, often violent and incoherent, but in the main com-
prehensible, against the dangers of an unprecedented
economic depression.

"Had it achieved its object, it would be difficult indeed
to criticize it; but facts are to hand which prove that
this exaggerated policy of protectionism, spreading from
one country to another, is tending to prolong the depression which it was designed to combat and to preju-
dice the interests of the classes that it aimed at protecting." [5]

Accumulation of New Surpluses

Once again war has intervened to cut off what inter-
change between the agricultural countries of the New
World and the industrial countries of continental Europe had survived the years of economic nationalism.
The League economists, reporting on world developments, are again drawing attention to the mounting
stocks of many agricultural commodities. It may well
be true that, after two years of war, the food situation
in Germany is much better than it was in 1916.[6] It

[5] League of Nations Economic Committee, *Considerations on the
Present Evolution of Agricultural Protectionism* (C.178.M.97.1935.
II.B.) (Geneva, 1935), pp. 6–7.

[6] Karl Brandt, "Food as a Political Instrument in Europe," and
"How Europe is Fighting Famine," *Foreign Affairs* (April and
July, 1941).

seems to have been good enough last winter "to allow of a consumption of calories not materially different from that of a working class family before the war," though the diet is "much reduced in proteins, vitamins and other protective foods." [7] Energy-producing foods were short during the winter of 1940–41 in Poland, Belgium, parts of France and Norway, and in Finland; and "these same countries, and especially Poland, would appear to have suffered most from insufficiency of vitamins and mineral salts." The area of deficiency was widely extended in the winter of 1941–42. Greece particularly suffered intensely. What future winters hold in store for these peoples cannot be accurately forecast; but it would seem probable that, despite German organizing energy, the increasing difficulties of transport and the overrunning of great food-producing areas such as the Ukraine must bring once more a great diminution of food supplies.

Meantime, surplus stocks cause increasing concern in overseas countries. The four major wheat-exporting countries alone had 1,116 million bushels in hand at the end of July, 1941. The approximate surplus expected by July, 1942, has been estimated at 1,500 million bushels.[8] The surplus of cotton stocks in July, 1941, was estimated at 20,454,000 bales, of which 12,692,000 were in the United States. Other great

[7] League of Nations, *World Economic Survey 1939–41* (Geneva, 1941).
[8] Leslie A. Wheeler, "Agricultural Surpluses in the Post-War World," *Foreign Affairs* (October, 1941).

though scattered surpluses exist and are increasing in vegetable-oil materials (copra, peanuts, linseed, etc.); in cocoa, tea, coffee, sugar, maize, silk, and tobacco; while perishable foods, such as frozen meats and butter, are taxing warehouse facilities in countries like New Zealand and Argentina because of the losses of refrigerated shipping tonnage. Even wool, so much in demand for military uniforms, is accumulating in Australia.

This story of shortages on one side and surplus stocks on the other is familiar from the experience of the first World War; but the surpluses are now much greater and more burdensome as a result of the protective policies pursued in the years between the wars. A new element has entered into the situation in the firmer authority now exercised by national governments over the rationing of consumption on the one hand and the effective control of surpluses by government intervention on the other.[9] A recent Australian official statement goes so far as to claim that

"we have carried the problem of stabilising primary production a stage further than any plans hitherto

[9] *Cf.* the long list of government controls recorded in successive issues of *Foreign Agriculture*, especially "Wartime Agricultural Policy of Canada," Vol. III, No. 12 (December, 1939), p. 593; "The Australian Wheat Industry Assistance Scheme," Vol. III, No. 11 (November, 1939), p. 509; "Agricultural Price Control in Foreign Countries," Vol. III, No. 2 (February, 1939), p. 45; "Canada's Wartime Agricultural Measures," Vol. IV, No. 6 (June, 1940), p. 333; "Rationing in the United Kingdom," Vol. V, No. 1 (January, 1941), p. 13; "Wartime Policies and Controls Affecting Agricultural Trade," Vol. V, No. 5 (May, 1941), p. 175.

adopted in Australia. It is a coordinated effort to place in reserve surplus export products whether in the form of stocks or processed goods and it will have a profound effect on plans for stabilising primary production in the difficulties which we will face after the war. Here is another installment of the Government's efforts to lay now the foundations of a more solid economic structure after the war. We are not waiting on the development of plans for a new world—we are building that world here and now."

International Commodity Controls

Moreover, national action has already led to international discussions and in certain fields to international action. Commodity-control agreements were in force before the war in respect to certain products, such as tin, rubber, wheat, and sugar. Summarizing a rapid survey of the problem of agricultural surpluses at the present time, an official of the United States Department of Agriculture draws four conclusions: that a marked disequilibrium existed before the war, that national efforts to remedy this disequilibrium had proved ineffective, that numerous efforts had been made "with varying degrees of success" to achieve regulation by international agreement, and that "the war has greatly aggravated the situation affecting these chronic surpluses. Huge stocks, out of all proportion to the amounts that move normally in international trade, will be piled up in the exporting countries when the war ends. To throw these stocks on the market would be disastrous." [10]

It may be remarked in passing that the new agricultural program launched by the United States Government in connection with lease-lend aid to Britain seems destined to extend the range of commodities in which surpluses may be accumulated. The prime need of Britain is for fats and protective foods. The farmers of the United States are, therefore, being urged to run the risk of overproduction after the war in order to provide exports of such products as butter, animal fat, and eggs. At the same time, it is made clear that any such overproduction can well be absorbed by measures to raise living standards and improve nutrition. [11] On the other hand, the extension of an imperial system of exchange control makes at least possible the replacement of American by Australian canned and dried fruits. It seems likely, therefore, that not only the staples, wheat, cotton, sugar, coffee, but a very wide range of agricultural foods and raw materials may need to be brought within the ambit of international control schemes.

Such schemes are already in preparation, and in them, for the first time, consideration for the consuming as well as the producing countries appears to be contemplated. The Inter-American Coffee Agreement entrusts

[10] Leslie A. Wheeler, *op. cit.*, p. 95.
[11] Statement of Secretary of Agriculture Wickard quoted in *New York Times* (November 14, 1941), p. 3.

the regulation of the market for a surplus commodity to the importing as well as the exporting countries, since it arranges "not only for export quotas, but also arranges that the largest consumer, the United States, shall make enforcement effective by the strict regulation of imports according to quotas." [12] A distinction should be drawn, however, between consuming countries and the ultimate consumers in those countries. Unless care is taken to safeguard the interests of the consumer, international commodity agreements may well be made at his expense.

There is likely, however, to be a more revolutionary development than those noted above. The beginnings of discriminating prices, somewhat analogous to the Food Stamp plan in the United States, are already in evidence. In July, 1941, an international wheat meeting "drafted the first major international commodity agreement written in anticipation of postwar needs," and, in doing so, expressed the hope that "by the establishment of an ever-normal granary and a large pool of relief wheat, the consumers of the world may be guaranteed abundant postwar supplies at prices reasonable both to them and to producers and free of charge to those in need of relief." [13]

---

[12] Wheeler, *op. cit.*, p. 94. It should be noted, however, that this arrangement entailed the necessity for introducing import quotas, which is difficult to reconcile with the principle of "equality of trading opportunity."

[13] *Ibid.*, p. 89.

This is a far cry indeed from the situation after the last war. The French and other plans for continuation of commodity controls then drawn up, largely as a means of economic constraint directed against a beaten enemy, were vetoed in advance by the United States not only in order to obtain justice in distribution, but also so that United States exporters could get adequate prices.

There are difficult problems to be faced in the negotiation of international commodity agreements, leading perhaps to the creation of great international control institutes. It is by no means certain that they can be organized in such a way as to solve rather than aggravate the problem of surpluses. The incorporation of consumer interests in the machinery of control is, however, a great step in advance. It may perhaps be hoped that such machinery can be created to function effectively in the immediate postwar period.

The Ultimate Causes of Disequilibrium

After the last war the shortage of foodstuffs and raw materials in Europe was sufficient to absorb the accumulated surpluses overseas. The process of absorption by competitive marketing led first to soaring scarcity prices and then to a precipitate decline. Continuance of control over an adequate transition period may possibly avert the necessity for traversing again this destructive and wasteful experience of boom and slump. It cannot avert the necessity for equating supply to demand.

But there remains a more delicate and difficult problem—perhaps the most crucial problem of international adjustment after the war—a problem that was never faced after the last war and ultimately proved to be the most obstinate cause of continuing disequilibrium. This problem has been hinted at in the statement of an American official that:

"There also is good reason for us to prepare now to make certain reasonable demands upon the Central European nations before they begin their task of postwar agricultural reconstruction. The problem of how to handle the world's wheat and sugar surpluses would be appreciably diminished if the costly and inefficient production of them could be limited or abolished. The people of the nations concerned would benefit from lower costs, and their fields could be used advantageously to remedy the deficiencies which exist in dairy products and other protective foods.

"No one would seriously suggest that these war-scarred and weakened nations should be compelled to give up prewar cultivation patterns and then be left merely with an admonition to produce something else. They are going to need help. But when we make our plans to give them financial and technical aid after the war, we should place emphasis on increasing their production of protective foods and discourage uneconomic efforts to establish trade isolationism." [14]

[14] *Ibid.*, pp. 100–101.

It is very desirable that this problem should be frankly faced in its political, as well as its economic, implications, and in other countries as well as those of central Europe. Essentially the problem lies in the use of political measures to protect economic activity that is unable without such aid to cope effectively with external competition. Even more dangerously, it lies in the political power that accrues to interest groups as they mobilize for their own protection.

The most extreme examples of such groups are naturally to be found in the older countries, where feudal landowners have managed to preserve many of their medieval privileges. But the danger is widespread. Resistance to economic adaptation as world conditions have changed has been stubborn on the part of peasant agriculturists in most European countries. It has been equally stubborn among the farming communities of the United States.

In the confusion and disintegration that followed the breakdown of exchange equilibrium in 1931, extraordinary measures of protection were devised in the form of quotas and exchange-control systems as well as tariffs. Behind these emergency barriers agricultural production has greatly increased, even though at high cost. To restore the interdependent trading of the predepression world calls for the reduction not only of economic protection but also of powerful political lobbies. It is improbable that merely negative action will suffice to achieve these objectives. Positive action to change the methods of agricultural production and direct them toward new objectives is also needed. A bold attack, however, is necessary to destroy the bastions of privilege.

German Agrarian Protection

That necessity may be illustrated summarily and bluntly by reference to the history of agricultural protectionism in Germany.[15] It goes back at least to 1879. The German Reich, established under the leadership of Prussia, had inherited the low-tariff policy of the liberal Zollverein. It was Bismarck's aim not only to initiate a high-protective policy to stimulate industrial development, but also to shift his political support from a parliamentary majority based on the liberal center to one based on the conservative right. Germany had been a grain-exporting country; and the agricultural interests, including the great landowners east of the Elbe, had been vehement supporters of the low-tariff policy.

The opening up of new grain-exporting areas, particularly in the Middle West of the United States, changed the situation of the great landowners almost

[15] For the summary which follows I am indebted to an unpublished MS. by Dr. Alexander Gerschenkron, entitled "Agricultural Protection and Democracy in Germany." For convenient brief historical accounts in English of the German policies of agricultural protectionism, cf. also League of Nations Economic Committee, op. cit., and Wilhelm Röpke, German Commercial Policy (London, 1934), chs. 6–8.

overnight. In a very few years after the severe crisis of 1873, German graingrowers not only lost their export markets, but also became a high-cost area threatened by constantly cheapening American wheat even in their own home markets. Continental Europe and Germany in particular never accepted the economic consequences of this great agricultural revolution. Britain did, and sacrificed the growing of grain in order to take advantage of the cheap food for its urban masses of industrial workers. Denmark, Belgium, Holland, and, for some decades, Switzerland, followed the same course and reaped the same advantage in lowered costs of industrial and agricultural manufactures. Their agriculture, after an initial period of adjustment, settled down to the production of perishable foods for the growing towns. The advent of refrigeration in the eighteen nineties increased the range of overseas agricultural competition and intensified the resistance of most Continental countries to the creation of a specialized, interdependent world agriculture.

By embarking in 1879 upon a high-protective policy, based upon the famous "compact of iron and rye," Bismarck did much more than resist economic change. He anchored the effective control of political power upon a combination between heavy industry and the feudal landowners in opposition to the growing strength of the urban proletariat. Democratic government, which inevitably rests largely upon the development of a responsible trading middle class and an or-

ganized labor movement, was thwarted, as it was meant
to be thwarted, by this shift of political power. Agrarian mysticism, the mysticism of blood and soil and
race, the exaltation of rural virtues in contrast with the
"godless" Social-Democratic movement and the "Jewish" capitalist-traders, antedates the Nazis, and has
merely been adopted by them. As early as the eighteen
nineties there was widespread propaganda for agricultural self-sufficiency, particularly as a measure of war
preparedness. It was nurtured by the protection of
agriculture in inefficient, high-cost areas whose leadership has always been provided by the most persistent
remnant of medieval feudalism in Europe, the Junker
landowning, aristocratic, and military caste of eastern
Prussia. Once entrenched, they have never yielded
power, and have known how to withstand such re-
formist plans as the resettlement schemes of the Social-
Democrats during the nineteen twenties. Even Hitler
had to modify his program of land settlement. The
militarists have known how to co-operate with and
use such adventurers as the Nazi leaders, as the latter
have known how to enlist the support of the Junkers.

It is a tragic error to believe that the defeat of Hit-
lerism, essential as it is, will root out the militarist spirit
from its German stronghold. No German chancellor,
of any party, has ever been able to touch the citadel
of their power, the protection of graingrowing in large
estates on unsuitable soils. Caprivi attempted it when
he negotiated a series of bilateral trade treaties in the

early eighteen nineties, but he was driven from power. German agricultural protectionism remained one of the chief obstacles to world trade and to peace up till the war of 1914–18.

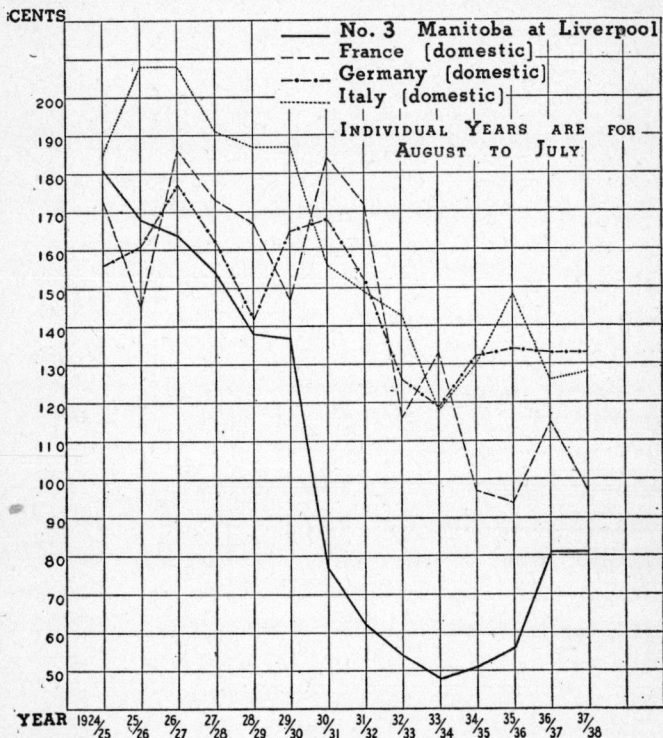

FIGURE 6

Annual average prices of imported and domestic wheat in Europe (United States pre-devaluation gold cents per bushel).

ANNUAL AVERAGE PRICES OF IMPORT AND
DOMESTIC WHEAT IN EUROPE
1924–1938 *

(U. S. pre-devaluation gold cents per bushel)

YEAR AUG.– JULY	UNITED KINGDOM (IMPORT) (NO. 3 MANITOBA)	FRANCE (DOMESTIC)	GERMANY (DOMESTIC)	ITALY (DOMESTIC)
1924–25	181	173	156	185
1925–26	168	145	161	208
1926–27	164	186	177	208
1927–28	154	173	162	191
1928–29	138	167	142	187
1929–30	137	147	165	187
1930–31	77	184	168	156
1931–32	62	172	152	149
1932–33	54	116	126	143
1933–34	48	133	119	118
1934–35	51	97	132	130
1935–36	56	94	134	148
1936–37	81	115	133	116
1937–38	81	97	133	118

* Source: *Wheat Studies of the Food Research Institute, Stanford University, California.*

Defeat in that war brought the necessity for great imports of food and raw materials. For a number of years Germany remained a free-trade area in grains. Yet until 1920 the high prices on the world market, and in the following years the undervaluation of the mark in the process of inflation, provided sufficient protection for the German graingrowers.

After 1925, German agricultural protectionism began anew. It was primarily a protection for grain, and above all redounded to the benefit of the great landowners. But economic distress was widespread, and it became possible to swing the peasant masses behind the Junkers' policy. The tariff on wheat, which had been nil while Germany was under Allied control, had risen to RM 5.00 per quintal by January 1, 1929, and to RM 25.00 per quintal by January 1, 1934. Thereafter, the National Socialist government was in power and the regulation of wheat imports was pursued by other means, but the tariff remained. Meantime, the price of wheat in the Reich, even in 1934, was almost three times the price of wheat on the free market at Rotterdam.

Protection of High-cost Agriculture

There can be no durable solution to the problem of world agricultural surpluses if this situation is allowed to recur. And there is not likely to be any peace in

Europe if the political power of the feudal, militarist, landowning Junkers is not smashed.[16] They survived the defeat of the Kaiser, but they should not be allowed to survive the defeat of Hitler. An effective sapping of their power, which has been largely responsible for the nationalist policies that have plunged the world into major wars twice in a generation, involves the destruction of their privileged economic position based upon the arbitrary and excessive protection of grain, wheat and rye. Some part of the lighter soils in eastern Germany ought really to go back to forest use. Other and better soils should be distributed in small holdings, primarily for dairying organized along co-operative lines.

The case of the Junkers is very clear, but it does not stand alone. With them should go the remaining feudal elements of Europe, such as the great landowners in Poland and Hungary. Agrarian reform, redistribution of the land, such as occurred in several European countries after the last war, is an essential basis for democracy and peaceful co-operation.[17] Moreover, the peasant farming of many democratic European countries is highly protected also, and the political power of the

[16] It should be emphasized also that economic nationalism in Germany rested on the compact of "iron and rye." The responsibility of the great industrialists both for aggressive protectionism and for the financing of the Nazi movement should not be forgotten. Thyssen, as well as Papen and Hindenburg, opened Hitler's way to power.

[17] Cf. the statement of Count Carlo Sforza in the *New York Times* (November 15, 1941), p. 14.

peasant parties rests on that protection. The extension of Soviet influence over much of central and eastern Europe may provide a drastic solution of this problem.

It is recognized that the suggestions contained in the preceding paragraph may seem to conflict with the third point of the Atlantic Charter, pledging the United Nations not to interfere with the rights of all peoples to choose their own form of government.[18] But it is obvious from many official statements that interference in national economic policy is now accepted as necessary to establish and maintain international economic equilibrium. It is an ostrichlike policy to pretend that economic interference does not have political implications. It is equally unrealistic to believe that nations can be allowed to choose their own forms of government with no respect for international standards of behavior and then be expected to follow the economic policies compatible with international equilibrium. If the statement of the Atlantic Charter means national autonomy within the limits of known and stated canons of political freedom and economic co-operation, it is clear that the particular form of administrative machinery can and ought to be left to local decision. But if world order is to be maintained it should be frankly recognized that economic sanctions, and behind them political sanctions, must be held in reserve if particular nations attempt to thwart the will of the world com-

[18] *See* p. 64, Chapter III of this book.

munity to peace and co-operation. If this constitutes interference in national political organization, it should be recognized that there can be no guarantee of peaceful co-operation without such interference. All modern wars are in some degree civil wars and, as events in Spain so amply demonstrated, no civil war can now be fought without international complications.

It should be emphasized that any country which perpetuates an area of high-cost production because of the political influence of those engaged in it, or the social importance attached to the preservation of the industry, runs grave risks of endangering democratic government. Political feeling always runs high in such cases. There are, perhaps, few cases in democratic countries where a powerful group interest has developed a political creed at all comparable with the agrarian mysticism that supports the feudal leadership of the German Junkers. It should be noted, however, that in some industries the United States is now at the crossroads of tariff policy that Germany reached in 1879. Certain products, of which wool is one, have now entered the category of high-cost production, and maintain their prices in this country out of equilibrium with those in other producing areas primarily by means of high-tariff protection. A breach has been made in this protection by the reduction in the duties on crossbred wools contained in the recent reciprocal trade agreement with Argentina; but the cost of maintaining the remaining duties, which are particularly high on fine wools, is heavy upon the American consumer and a stumbling block to trade with other countries.

Resistance to any reduction of such duties or to the removal of veterinary embargoes, such as that on imports of chilled and frozen meat, is very strong. The sugar lobby is also powerful, though beet sugar is clearly a high-cost industry on the mainland of the United States.

Reduction of such impediments to freer international trade would clearly involve property losses, for example, in land values, just as reduced support to the prices of other farm products, such as cotton, would involve financial losses though not necessarily to the actual growers. A democracy needs to be aware of the political dangers, as well as the economic costs, involved in protecting such areas of high-cost production.

Need for Improved Nutrition

It remains only to point out that a promising line of attack upon this problem of agricultural surpluses has been opened up by the effort to diversify production and direct it to supplying local markets with the commodities needed to assure reasonable living standards. This effort, which promises to ease the transitional costs of readjustment where high-cost production has been maintained or even stimulated by excessive protection, is consistent with the trend of political thought and action toward the assertion of every citizen's right to a greater measure of social security. It is also consistent with "the newer knowledge of nutrition" which emphasizes the value of protective foods, most of which are perishable and best produced in areas adjacent to their main markets. It builds, therefore, upon the principle stated above, that international co-operation must for the future be based upon economic policies designed to maximize purchasing power.

Of the many actions in democratic countries which have already been taken in this direction, it is perhaps sufficient, for illustration, to recall that the Agricultural Adjustment Administration in the United States, especially in its most recent phases, is primarily a plan to diversify production and make possible improved nutrition. The Tennessee Valley Authority also has been designed, in part, to promote more diversified agriculture (as well as industrial development) over a wide area at present devoted largely to the production of one staple crop, cotton, that has for many years suffered from chronic surpluses.

The experience gained in Britain during the enforced rationing of the present war is not likely to be lost. As Sir John Orr has shown, all but the poorest of the population of Britain before the war were able to secure enough proteins, though perhaps 10 per cent had insufficient fat. The diet of a much larger percentage was insufficient in the vitamins as well as in calcium, iron, and phosphorus. Faulty purchasing and inadequate dietary knowledge account for some part of this malnutrition; but the major cause is poverty. Improved nutrition is not merely a problem of education and public health, but "a part of the wider problem of raising the general standard of living."

Sir John Orr has calculated that "raising the food consumption of the whole population to the level of the top 10 per cent who buy nutritionally satisfactory diets, would involve an increase in the demand for milk of 80 per cent, for butter of 41 per cent, for eggs of 55 per cent, for meat of 29 per cent, for fruit of 124 per cent and for vegetables of 87 per cent." [19]

Even in the United States, nutrition surveys have revealed the prevalence of inadequate diets among a much larger section of the population than is commonly supposed.[20] For the most part, the problem in the United States, as in most of the British Dominions and the highly industrialized western European countries, is not a lack of energy-producing foods so much as insufficient use of the more expensive protective foods—meat, milk, butter, eggs, and citrus fruits. There is, however, in every country, a fairly substantial low-income group which has a struggle to get sufficient

[19] John Boyd Orr, *Food, Health and Income* (London, 1936).
[20] Cf. League of Nations, *Final Report of the Mixed Committee of the League of Nations on the Relation of Nutrition to Health, Agriculture and Economic Policy*, A.13.1937.II.A (Geneva, 1937), pp. 297–306.

energy-producing foods. If this is so in the richer countries, it is more obviously true in the industrially undeveloped countries. The nutrition surveys undertaken in connection with the League of Nations campaign have revealed the essential poverty of large masses of the world's population.[21]

It is, after all, the merest common sense as well as sound economics to build up the efficiency, productive capacity, and purchasing power of populations at present sunk in the morass of poverty caused by the pressure of population on limited productive resources. The only possible way to raise consumption levels and living standards among these peoples is to increase their productive capacity. To do this, great projects of industrialization are ultimately called for. That industrial development can work wonders has been demonstrated by the U.S.S.R. But there is no need to go through the agony of revolution to achieve industrialization. Freer trade and investment worked this miracle in the nine-

[21] *Cf.* League of Nations, *op. cit.;* also League of Nations, European Conference on Rural Life, Geneva, 1939; and League of Nations Health Organization, Intergovernmental Conference of Far Eastern Countries on Rural Hygiene, Geneva, 1937. Of Asia the League of Nations Health Organization reported that "it is thought that of the 1,150,000,000 inhabitants of that continent not less than 75% have a diet below the standards fixed by European science. . . . It appears that a large part of the population is living on the borderline of the minimum requirements, while millions are even below that level." League of Nations, Health Organization, Intergovernmental Conference of Far Eastern Countries on Rural Hygiene, Report by the Preparatory Committee, document C.H.1234. Ser.L.1.N.P.1937.III.3 (Geneva, 1937).

teenth century. The New World countries developed in that century, however, drew energy and initiative from abundant food supplies. The first need of the industrially backward populations of the world at the present time is sufficient food. If this need were even approximately met, there would be no agricultural surpluses to dispose of.

"The achievement of a satisfactory level of nutrition," in the words of Mr. F. L. McDougall, who was largely responsible for initiating the League of Nations campaign in this field, "makes two primary demands, namely the capacity of agriculture to produce more food, in particular, more dairy products, eggs, fruit and vegetables, and the provision of some at least of these foods, whether energy or protective, at lower prices so that the less well-off sections of populations may find an adequate dietary within reach of their incomes." [22]

Campaigns for improved nutrition, better housing, and improved living standards generally [23] may have a better chance of success after this war in so far as readiness to experiment with such policies is concerned; though they cannot be regarded as dispensing with the necessity for a more direct attack upon the obstacles now barring the way to international economic cooperation. There is no easy road back to peace and

[22] F. L. McDougall, *Food and Welfare* (Geneva, 1938).
[23] *Cf.* N. F. Hall, *Preliminary Investigation into Measures of a National or International Character for Raising the Standard of Living* (Geneva, 1938).

prosperity; but it is even truer today than when Mr. McDougall wrote in November, 1938, that "the five aims of an improved level of nutrition, higher standards of living, a more prosperous agriculture, freer international trade and an increased volume of trade, together interlock to form lines of policy which should ensure economic and political stability to the nations prepared for such co-operation and if vigorously prosecuted should help to promote the peace so desirable but so difficult of achievement in the world today." [24]

[24] F. L. McDougall, *op. cit.*, p. 56.

CHAPTER VI

DEBT AND
DEMOBILIZATION

The Lessons of Mobilization

IN CONSIDERING a possible change-back from war to
peace production, the experience of recent months
when peace production was being changed over to war
purposes must be kept in mind. The problems are real.
That is to say, they consist primarily of difficulties arising in the transference of workers from industry to
industry and from district to district; difficulties also
in regard to surpluses and shortages of important raw
materials. In many ways the most awkward difficulties,
however, arise on the side of capital equipment.
Specialized factories for particular purposes prove difficult of adaptation and in any event require expensive
and prolonged retooling. Excess capacity may have
existed on a great scale just before the present war
broke out, but it did not prove easy to utilize for the
production of goods of a different sort.[1] The Ger-

[1] For detailed discussion of the problems raised in this section,
cf. Seymour E. Harris, *The Economics of American Defense* (New
York, 1941), especially ch. 14.

mans who in peace prepared for war had a much easier problem of mobilization.[2]

These problems of labor mobility and training, raw-material priorities, and capital adaptation for war production are by now very clear. It is equally clear that the monetary and fiscal policies by which the change-over is being financed have an important bearing on the real as well as the monetary costs of the defense program. In order to get the program under way, purchasing power must be made available for plant construction, raw-material purchases, and wage payments. Before the United States defense program got into its stride, for example, urgently needed plant extension had in many instances to be financed by the British Purchasing Commission, which in some cases not only contracted to buy the output, but advanced the working and even the fixed capital. As the United States program swung into effect, new production facilities were provided either by Treasury advances or by an extension of commercial bank loans to private industrialists.

Long before the defense program reached its production peak, shortages of strategic raw materials and even of certain types of skilled labor made their appearance. It became necessary, therefore, to allocate raw materials on a basis of priorities, so that the production of goods for civilian consumption was restricted.

[2] *Cf.* the examples given by Douglas Miller, *You Can't Do Business with Hitler* (New York, 1941), pp. 18–23.

The prospect (and widespread fear) of an inflationary rise of prices is due primarily to the increased purchasing power made available by enlarged profits and payrolls at a time when the supply of consumers' goods is being progressively restricted. It is obvious that commodity prices will rise, and indeed have already risen, as consumers with more money in their pockets compete for short supplies, particularly of durable consumers' goods.

The inequities caused by a sharp inflationary rise of prices are not to be denied. They cause a drastic redistribution of national income at the expense not of great but of small creditors and of fixed-income receivers. Farmers for a time gain higher prices for their products, but become involved in land speculation. Laborers gain higher wages but are soon faced by vast unemployment. The great mass of contributors to life insurance and pension funds lose part at least of their dearly bought security. The orderly routine of saving and investment is wrecked, and a premium is put on speculation rather than production. The worst damage of an inflation is done before it becomes uncontrollable, but inflation does not become uncontrollable until a community loses faith in its currency. Then, by getting rid of currency in a scramble for goods the public multiplies the effectiveness of the currency by causing a rapid rise in the velocity of circulation. There is a creeping inflation under way in many countries at the present time but it has nowhere reached the stage of hyperinflation, and this stage is certainly distant in the United States. Preoccupation with inflationary dangers and concern over a mounting public debt are both right and natural; but in the United States they seem to have failed to evoke acceptance of adequate controls.

Concern over the mounting public debt has so far reflected the shock of awakening from a privileged situation rather than any real danger of national bankruptcy. Britain, with just over forty million people, entered the war period with a national debt of about £8,500 millions, almost as great a burden as the United States carried before the war with three times as many people and more than three times Britain's annual productive capacity. The national debt of the United States is now increasing fast and it may not be long before it will approximate the burden that less fortunate communities have had to carry for generations. The size of the debt, up till the outbreak of war, reflected the fact that war costs and war preparations had been light in the past. Increased debt is inevitable when a great increase in such costs can no longer be avoided. The public debt, however, cannot go on increasing indefinitely, and when the war ends there will be good reason to arrest and even reverse the trend of increase.

It is common ground among financial experts that it is sound policy to gather back by taxation the purchasing power that has been created to finance the expan-

sion of production.[3] A sufficient and varied system of
taxation cannot, however, be imposed quickly enough
to prevent some inflationary rise of the price level, and
the sacrifices involved in heavier taxation must be
severe and must reach every section of the community
if consumption is to be effectively restricted. It is not
easy in a democracy to achieve sacrifices of this character.[4] Yet it should be clear that the greater the proportion of the costs of war that can be paid out of current
income, the less will be the disturbance of price and
wage levels, and the easier, therefore, will be the ensuing
problems of financing the demobilization period.

The Greater Difficulty of Demobilization

In many respects the change-back from war to peace
production is likely to be more difficult than the transition from peace to war. In practically every country
armament and even war expenditures began when the
national economy was far from full employment of
economic resources. There were millions of unemployed workers to be drawn into active production,

[3] Cf., e.g., the very clear statement by an Australian economist,
E. Ronald Walker, *War-Time Economics* (Melbourne, 1939),
ch. 5.

[4] Cf. J. M. Keynes, *How to Pay for the War* (London, 1940), p. 7:
"In a totalitarian state the problem of the distribution of sacrifice
does not exist. That is one of its initial advantages for war. It is
only in a free community that the task of government is complicated by the claims of social justice."

raw materials were abundant and low in price, and there was a good deal of unused productive capacity.

At the close of the war, these conditions are likely to be reversed, so that the problems of transition start from the disadvantageous point of having to create unemployment, control raw materials, and build new kinds of capital equipment because great armament factories have to go into obsolescence or on the scrap heap. A change-over to different types of production is obviously more difficult at the top of a great investment boom than at the depression stage of the business cycle. Resistance to adaptation is least when productivity is expanding and greatest when it is contracting.

There will be, of course, a backlog of unfilled demand. Automobiles will be older, transport equipment will need repairs and replacements, housing will have fallen behind. In some countries these demands may be of compelling and even tragic urgency. But, if uncontrolled, as after previous wars, this condition may merely lead to a scramble for the limited civilian goods that are available, with a steep rise of prices soon brought to a sudden and calamitous halt when the demobilization of the war industries brings unemployment and reduced purchasing power.

It would seem the path of wisdom, therefore, for the democratic countries to take advantage of this period of the replacement boom to reduce armament expenditures as quickly as workers and resources can be transferred into expanding civilian production. It is also desirable, even necessary, to keep firm control of scarce raw materials and to distribute them in such a manner as will minimize the upward pressure on prices and facilitate the transition from war to peace industries. The extent to which this double line of policy can be followed without inflationary risks will be determined largely by the extent to which the actual war and defense programs have been paid for by drastic taxation of current income.

Similarly, the launching and rapid expansion of a program of civilian construction when the first replacement demands begin to dwindle will be facilitated if government credit remains unimpaired by excessive borrowing. In this connection, it should be recalled that not only the size but the composition of the national debt must be borne in mind. A large debt is in itself an obstacle to further large government expenditure that must be borrowed from private savings or from created credit. If the debt is not only large, but largely composed of short- and medium-term borrowings rather than consolidated long-term securities, the obstacle is much more serious.[5] It is important, therefore, that in addition to heavy taxation, as large a proportion as possible of the borrowing in time of war shall be from private savings or unused balances, and that the borrowing shall as far as possible be on long-term.

[5] The heavy debt burden of Great Britain after the last war offers instructive experience on this point. *Cf.* N. F. Hall, *The Exchange Equalization Account* (London, 1935), ch. 2.

These considerations are important if, as seems almost certain to be the case, national governments attempt to ward off depression and unemployment when depression threatens, by financing great public works and launching programs of urban development designed to promote rehousing. The less overborrowed the government is, and the less its indebtedness is in the form of short-dated securities, the greater will be the available private funds, and the easier it will be to issue further securities in prosecution of peace plans without direct inflationary creation of new bank credit. In any case, governments with unbalanced budgets and large debts carried at relatively low interest rates are tempted to keep those rates at a low level in order to minimize their budgetary deficits. With great unsatisfied civilian demands and very low interest rates, the danger of heavy private borrowing creating an inflationary boom becomes very real. There is some danger of forgetting that credit and debt are two aspects of the same transaction.

Planning for Postwar Employment

If it is presumed that national governments will attempt to launch public works and schemes of urban reorganization to take up the slack of employment when the replacement boom shows signs of coming to an end, it is the path of wisdom to prepare such schemes in advance and to direct them so that they facilitate rather than impede adaptation to the changed international economic situation that may be expected after the war. This points, in the first place, to a damping down of normal peacetime expenditures during the war emergency, a course that is in any case dictated by the necessity of mobilizing labor and materials for maximum war production.

A great deal of preliminary planning can be done in respect of postwar employment by private firms and corporations, by local bodies, state and federal departments.[6] There is much temptation, especially to local bodies and state departments, to use their improved financial situation to reduce taxation and increase expenditure. This not only adds fuel to the inflationary fire now, but may well thwart much needed reconstruction programs after the war.

Many state and local governments have seen their financial situation immensely improved by the expenditure by federal funds in their areas. Deficits have in some cases been converted into surpluses. In most areas, relief expenditure has dwindled and receipts from existing taxes have increased. It would be prudent to repay debt, bank up balances, and improve state credit by

[6] *Cf.* The Tenth Fortune Round Table, "On Demobilizing the War Economy" (September 5, 6, 7, 1941). Also David C. Prince, "Post-Defense Readjustments," Construction and Civic Development Department, Chamber of Commerce of the United States (Washington, D.C., 1941).

maintaining taxes and economizing expenditure against the time, perhaps not so far distant, when demands on the local and state treasuries will again become urgent.

The preparation of detailed plans for the postwar period is necessarily a matter for experts with detailed and local knowledge of possible developments and probable needs. All that can be stated as a general principle is the desirability of having such plans in hand and the necessity of so preparing the financial situation that at the critical moment savings are available to launch the new programs as war industry is gradually cut down.

Such preparations are under way, particularly in the field of housing, but more than central-government action is needed if the vitality of local government as well as private enterprise is to be preserved. The experience of the long depression and the slow recovery in many countries between 1929 and 1936 is sufficient evidence that even large-scale central-government expenditure cannot take the place of paralyzed private and local-government initiative. In particular, building accounts for such a substantial proportion of new capital investment that government action should be directed toward creating the possibility for a great development of private building when the first replacement boom slackens. To do this, costs must be reduced, interest rates kept low, monopolistic and restrictive material and labor costs combated, land made available by clearance schemes, and community facilities provided by road, water, electrical, and drainage-works programs.

It should be emphasized that the promotion of postwar schemes for civilian employment is primarily a problem for each national community to solve within its own borders. The solution in great industrial countries can probably best be found by a judicious reliance on private enterprise for the production of durable consumers' goods, supplemented by government action in regard to public works calling for heavy investment and creating demand for producers' goods. Even if such public works are undertaken, the lessened needs for steel, machinery, and machine tools consequent upon demobilization of war production may well create a crisis in the basic heavy industries. Some relief may be given to those industries if international reconstruction plans can be devised to speed the modern development of countries such as China, India, some countries of Latin America, and much of eastern Europe, which at present lack effective transport and industrial equipment and the capital with which to produce them. Something is said later concerning the possibilities of such plans; but it would be a mistake not to stress the fact that the major solutions for the postwar employment problem must be found at home, in the national economies of the great industrial countries themselves.

This is true, above all, of the United States. From many points of view the maintenance of employment and national income in the United States, and to a less extent in Great Britain, is the key to the whole world problem. Within the British Commonwealth and the so-called sterling area, the maintenance of employment and purchasing power will depend substantially upon the ability of the Dominions and Colonies to export steadily at satisfactory prices, mainly to Great Britain and the United States. Their power to import and to maintain local production is very directly dependent upon their export receipts. When the United States buys raw materials heavily, the raw-material-producing countries buy more from Europe and especially from Great Britain, which in turn can buy more raw materials for its own industries. The recovery of these countries, therefore, depends largely upon production and employment being maintained at a high level in the United States and Great Britain.

Great Britain itself will be in a much less favorable position on international account than it has been for more than a century.[7] The hope of British recovery

[7] Cf. Geoffrey Crowther, "Anglo-American Pitfalls," *Foreign Affairs* (October, 1941), pp. 10–11: "Great Britain's factories are being bombed (not very extensively, it is true); the British mercantile marine is being sunk; British foreign trade connections are being disrupted; British reserves of gold and investments have been exhausted. It is almost certain that the pound sterling will be weakened and the dollar strengthened by the war, and that the sterling area will have even greater difficulty than before the war in obtaining a sufficient supply of dollars. Moreover, there is the factor of possible repayment of Lease-Lend borrowings to be taken into account. It has been suggested by more than one in the United States that Britain might make repayment in tin and rubber. In

must, therefore, be intimately linked with the possibility that "the level of domestic prosperity in the United States may be so high that American purchases of British goods will be substantially higher than before the war." [8]

A strong and prosperous United States is the most important contribution that Americans can make to the reorganization of the postwar world; but the United States cannot be strong and prosperous unless it shares actively in reorganizing the prosperity and strength of other countries. American manufacturing activity was calculated, even before the war, to account for about 45 per cent of the world total.[9] Immediately after the war this figure will certainly be higher.

The demand of the United States for raw materials and for a variety of manufactured imports is a potent factor in determining the ability of other countries to maintain their national incomes, and their demands help to sustain income in the United States. The swing of the business cycle in a country that buys such huge quantities of raw materials in world markets cannot be ignored. When the United States is prosperous, the world has at least a chance to prosper with it. The first necessity of postwar reconstruction, therefore, is to restore flexible peacetime equilibrium between costs

---

general it is a just and reasonable suggestion. But it would vastly increase the scarcity of dollars throughout the sterling area."

[8] *Ibid.*, p. 12.

[9] *Cf.* League of Nations, *World Production and Prices 1935–36* (Geneva, 1936), p. 22.

and prices in the United States, so as to ward off the danger of an inflationary boom and consequent slump, such as followed the last war. If such a desirable end can be achieved, the world may escape the unfortunate retreat toward economic isolation represented by the higher tariffs to which the United States had recourse in each of the great depressions following 1918—the Fordney-McCumber tariff in 1922 and the Hawley-Smoot tariff in 1930.

It does not necessarily follow that a prosperous United States, even if it lowers its tariff by an extension of the Reciprocal Trade Agreement program, will be able to forestall severe depression and restrictive policies in other countries; but it will at least be in a position to take effective action to assist those of its neighbors who wish to follow policies of expanding prosperity rather than restriction.

Co-ordination of National Policies

Sound national economic policies, however, while the indispensable foundation for international cooperation, are not enough in themselves. It is improbable that a stable monetary equilibrium and an expanding system of multilateral trade can be established except on the basis of national economic policies so designed as to achieve an approximation to full employment of all national resources—not of labor only.

But if such national policies are pursued in spite of their international consequences, they will not only present insuperable obstacles to the achievement of international economic co-operation; they will also fail to achieve their narrower purposes. Stable national prosperity is not attainable for any community except in a peaceful and prosperous world. A great deal can be achieved by unilateral measures of adaptation to the new circumstances; but unless national recovery plans are co-ordinated so as to minimize strain on the international balances of payments, there is grave risk of resort to economic nationalism of a restrictive character. The experience of national recovery plans in the last great depression is sufficient proof of this.

The easiest and surest way to ensure parallel development of national economic policies is by linking the leading currencies in agreement to maintain stability of the exchange rates and by pegging the currencies of smaller countries to one or another of the leaders. This does not mean a return to the gold standard; still less does it mean unilateral exchange stabilization by one country after another. But it does mean that no country should be allowed to determine the exchange value of its own currency or alter that value without consultation with other countries. The exchange rate of any currency is a ratio—its value in terms of another currency. The British monetary authorities have no more power to determine that £1 sterling shall be worth $4 than the United States authorities have to determine that $4 shall equal £1 sterling. Competitive exchange depreciation is the road to monetary chaos. Concerted action to ward off such beggar-my-neighbor policies is both wise and necessary.

Such concerted action has been taken in the past. By the Tripartite Agreement of September, 1936, the governments of the United States, Great Britain, and France (later joined by Belgium, Holland, and Switzerland) agreed "to maintain the greatest possible equilibrium in the system of international exchange and to avoid to the utmost extent the creation of any disturbance of that system" by national monetary action.[10] This agreement is still technically in force. So far as the United States and Great Britain are concerned, it is operative. Events have shown that its existence does not preclude an alteration of the external value of a currency that is under strain. The technique of exchange regulation is now better organized,[11] so that if sufficient reserves are available little difficulty is experienced in checking speculative attacks or forestalling panic flights of capital.

The broad outlines of a simple and workable mechanism of monetary co-operation would seem to be reasonably clear. The present or adjusted rates of exchange arrived at after expert consultation would be pegged

[10] Bank for International Settlements, "The Tripartite Agreement" (Basle, January, 1937).

[11] Cf. N. F. Hall, op. cit., and Leonard Waight, The History and Mechanism of the Exchange Equalization Account (Cambridge, 1939).

for an interim period by agreement among the United States, Great Britain, and such other countries as were parties to the agreement. The sterling currencies would continue to be pegged on the pound sterling, and many others, such as the Chinese yuan, on the dollar. Exchange equalization funds, working in consultation or through the medium of an International Bank endowed with sufficient gold and other exchange assets, would absorb temporary fluctuations around the agreed level.

It must be recognized that large liquid funds exist, the amount and distribution of which are not fully known. Precautions against the transfers' of such funds upsetting the exchanges must be maintained; but the origin of such funds is to be found largely in fear of exchange depreciation causing capital losses. The only real solution of the problem of "hot money" is the re-establishment of exchange stability.

In Chapter IX, something more is said of the problems that arise in connection with the change-over from economic warfare pivoted on exchange control to a freer multilateral trading system. It is evident that there must first be a period in which workable exchange rates are determined and national economic policies of adaptation to peace conditions are worked out. Once equilibrium is restored, it must be maintained by national policies running in parallel, so as to avoid undue strains on the international balances of payments.

It is very necessary that the international aspects of this problem of reorganizing national production shall be kept in mind. Any nation pursuing an expansionist national policy without regard for its international consequences would soon run into a choice between insulating itself from international disequilibria by autarkic measures, or allowing such disequilibria to wreck its national equilibrium. Only by a common and co-operative effort to reorganize an expanding prosperity can the ideal of full employment be approached.

CHAPTER VII

REPAYMENT AND REPARATION

The Legacy of World War I

AFTER the last war, negotiations for the repayment of
war debts incurred among the Allies proved to be a
fruitful source of misunderstanding and political bitter-
ness. Few problems were more destructive of co-
operative attitudes than that of the war debts. The
United States, where public opinion was opposed to
the exaction of reparation payments, steadily refused
to link them with payments on account of war debt.
In Britain, however, and even more in France, these
payments in and out were regarded as inextricably
linked.

The denomination of the war debts in monetary
terms and the calculation of compound interest payments swelled the amounts to unreal proportions. The
facts may be illustrated by a brief summary of the
figures regarding the British debt to the United States.
At the time of the debt-settlement negotiations in 1923,

Britain owed the United States a principal sum of $4,600 million.[1]

About $3,700 million had been borrowed between April 6, 1917, and November 11, 1918 (as against $3,-200 million which Britain lent her Allies in this period), and there were about $400 million of post-Armistice credits. Interest and adjustments in respect of these sums brought the net total outstanding at the time of the debt agreement in 1923 to the figure stated above, $4,600 million. The bulk of the loans was made at relatively high interest rates and was spent in the United States for the purchase of commodities at a time when prices were high. In the British view, they were spent in promoting a common cause.

At the close of the Armistice period, Britain was in the position of owing to the United States almost exactly what she was owed by her Allies. It was natural, therefore, that the British Government should propose an all-round cancellation. The French were in somewhat the same position, since debts to Britain and the United States were about balanced by reparation payments to be made by Germany. The cancellation proposal, however, attempted to set off debts which the United States regarded as sound against Allied payments to Britain and reparation payments to France that could only be regarded as hypothetical. In effect,

[1] Before the United States entered the war on April 6, 1917, Britain had borrowed about $1,000 million from private sources. In this period (1914–17) Britain lent her Allies $3,814 million, of which $1,657 million were borrowed by Tsarist Russia.

it became a suggestion that Germany should be excused from reparation payments if the United States would cancel the loans made to the Allies.[2] The original proposal for cancellation referred only to intergovernmental war debts, but the linking up with reparation payments was the inevitable result of France's situation. The proposal was rejected by the United States, and separate debt settlements were effected.

In the case of Great Britain the principal sum of $4,600 million was to be paid by installments over a period of sixty-two years, the compound interest over this period being calculated to amount to $6,500 million, making a gross total, including interest, of over $11,000 million. It is this gross total, about two and a half times the original sum borrowed, that is commonly referred to as being now in default. Of the amounts (totaling $1,352 million) paid by Britain to the United States between the funding of the loan in 1923 and the Hoover moratorium in July, 1931, $202 million went to reduction of principal and the remaining $1,150 million represented interest.[3]

There is no need to review here the controversy which, after the expiration of the Hoover moratorium, resulted first in a gold payment by Britain, then token

[2] Cf. Harold G. Moulton and Leo Pasvolsky, *War Debts and World Prosperity* (Washington, 1932); especially ch. 4.

[3] Including the payments made after the moratorium, Great Britain paid altogether $1,464 million. This is slightly more than 80 per cent of the total payments received from all countries owing war debts to the United States, though the British share of those debts was only 40 per cent of the total.

payments, and finally default. The reparation payments from Germany were in effect abandoned at the Lausanne Conference in July, 1932, and it was not many months before the bulk of the Allied debts to the United States was defaulted also. The United States continued until December, 1940, to send a formal note of payments due each half year, including interest on payments in arrears. The official bulletin of the Department of State contains no record of such reminders having been sent in June and December, 1941. This omission, after the passing of the Lease-Lend Act, has not been accompanied by any public intimation of a change in policy regarding the war debts and seems to have passed unnoticed. The State Department has no legal power to make a debt settlement. Whether its omission of the customary reminders of payments due is to be construed as tacit acceptance of the temporary necessity for default is undisclosed.

It seems obvious, however, that since reparation payments from Germany on account of the last war have been abandoned, and since the prospect is remote of either the United States or Britain effectively collecting any further payments on account of 1914–18 war debts from Russia, France, Italy, Belgium, Yugoslavia, Roumania, Greece, Czechoslovakia, Estonia, Latvia, Lithuania, Poland, or even Finland, and since, also, Great Britain's own international financial position has been weakened by the present war, the claims upon Great Britain must virtually be abandoned. Any payment that she may be able to make on account of war debts incurred before 1920 must either be nominal or else a payment in kind, such as cession of naval bases.

Lease-Lend Indebtedness

The situation is now complicated by the growth of indebtedness in kind represented by the increasing shipments, mainly to Great Britain, of armaments, food, materials, and other war needs, including ships and ship repairs, under the Lease-Lend legislation. The provisions of the Neutrality Act prohibited the issue of new loans to any belligerent, publicly or privately; but in providing the necessary dollars to pay cash for evergrowing purchases in the United States and even for the financing of new factories, Britain not only stripped herself of liquid foreign assets, but also depleted her capacity to earn such assets in the future. The adverse balance of payments on dollar account against Great Britain for the years 1940–41 was estimated "roughly as equal to the (British) dollar and gold assets available at the outbreak of war." [4] While lease-lend aid has taken care of some of this adverse balance and will do so to an increasing extent in the future, British exchange assets have already been depleted. Not all the

[4] *Cf.*, for a recent analysis of the strain on the British balance of payments, Seymour E. Harris, *The Economics of American Defense* (New York, 1941), ch. 12.

remaining assets are liquid.[5] Some readily marketable
securities have been sold and others mortgaged. A considerable part of the adverse balance has been paid by
shipments of gold. Increased deliveries of certain raw
materials, such as rubber, tin, and wool, have been made
at good prices. Britain has also run into debt to Canada,
and in less degree to other Dominions, on account of
war supplies, and this will reduce her importing capacity after the war.[6] It is of little use at this stage to
calculate either the amount of the new indebtedness
that has been and is being incurred on lease-lend account, or the depletion up till now of British earning
assets abroad.[7]

It does not require exact knowledge, however, to
grasp the fact that Britain's capacity to make a reasonable repayment on account of the materials supplied to
her for war purposes will depend largely upon what
earning assets she will have left after the war. The
transfer now to American holders of certain types of
British assets (debts owed by the Australian, Indian,

[5] Cf. ibid., p. 260: "A large part of these assets are salable only
at large sacrifices of price, if at all. Mr. Keynes estimates that of
£3,700 million of British foreign investments at the end of 1938,
about £3,000 million consisted of sterling loans and of shares of
companies registered in Great Britain, most of which could not be
realised. He estimates that over a period of three years only £250
million of these £3,000 million could be realised per year."

[6] On December 29, 1941, Canada canceled British obligations
amounting to $1,150 million. Cf. New York Times (December 30,
1941), p. 1.

[7] Cf. discussion of this problem in the Economist (November
22, 1941), p. 630, and (December 13, 1941), p. 712.

or other governments, or title to rubber plantations and tin mines in Malaya), or the acquisition by American investors of British-owned enterprises in the United States or South America might pay current bills, but it would reduce future capacity to pay. It would be using capital assets to pay for current consumption. Nor would it solve the prospective problem of securing dollar balances with which to pay the United States for future imports—a problem that is likely to confront every country, including Great Britain, after the war. It is not to the long-run interest of the United States so to weaken the international economic position of Great Britain that the latter must secure vital imports of foods and raw materials within an exchange-controlled trading area, for lack of dollar assets. Both in regard to payment and in regard to dollar transfers, Britain's capacity must be nursed if any hopes are to be entertained of restoring a greater measure of free multilateral trade after the war as a means of liquidating international obligations.

The magnitude of these problems has been greatly reduced by the character of the lease-lend legislation which, in the words of President Roosevelt, takes the dollar sign off the transaction. Monetary loans are not being made and therefore there is no question of interest payments compounding. Goods are being supplied. What valuation will in the future be placed upon ships that have been sunk, shells that have been fired, tanks that have been wrecked, or airplanes that have crashed is left to the discretion of the President of the United States—whoever he may be when the time of settlement arrives.[8]

On February 23, 1942, the governments of the United States and Great Britain signed an important agreement in pursuance of the provisions of the Lease-Lend Act of March 11, 1941. This agreement recognizes that it is still too early to define precise and detailed terms of repayment. But certain broad principles are laid down. It has long been evident that political agreement, particularly in regard to trade policy after the war, might well be an important part of the lease-lend settlement. The important Article VII of the recent agreement makes it clear that the British Government has committed itself to the multilateral trading policy advocated by the United States. The agreement is so important in this connection that it is reproduced herewith.[9]

"Article I. The Government of the United States of America will continue to supply the Government of the United Kingdom with such defense articles, defense services, and defense information as the President shall authorize to be transferred or provided.

[8] "The terms and conditions upon which any such foreign government receives any aid . . . shall be those which the President deems satisfactory and the benefit to the United States may be payment or repayment in kind or property, or any other direct or indirect benefit which the President deems satisfactory."

[9] Department of State, *Bulletin* (February 28, 1942), Vol. VI, No. 140, Publication 1700, pp. 191–92. Similar agreements have since been signed by the U.S.S.R. and China.

"Article II. The Government of the United Kingdom will continue to contribute to the defense of the United States of America and the strengthening thereof and will provide such articles, services, facilities or information as it may be in a position to supply.

"Article III. The Government of the United Kingdom will not without the consent of the President of the United States of America transfer title to, or possession of, any defense article or defense information transferred to it under the act or permit the use thereof by anyone not an officer, employee, or agent of the Government of the United Kingdom.

"Article IV. If, as a result of the transfer to the Government of the United Kingdom of any defense article or defense information, it becomes necessary for that Government to take any action or make any payment in order fully to protect any of the rights of a citizen of the United States of America who has patent rights in and to any such defense article or information, the Government of the United Kingdom will take such action or make such payment when requested to do so by the President of the United States of America.

"Article V. The Government of the United Kingdom will return to the United States of America at the end of the present emergency, as determined by the President, such defense articles transferred under this Agreement as shall not have been destroyed, lost or consumed and as shall be determined by the President to be useful in the defense of the United States of America or of the Western Hemisphere or to be otherwise of use to the United States of America.

"Article VI. In the final determination of the benefits to be provided to the United States of America by the Government of the United Kingdom full cognizance shall be taken of all property, services, information, facilities, or other benefits or considerations provided by the Government of the United Kingdom subsequent to March 11, 1941, and accepted or acknowledged by the President on behalf of the United States of America.

"Article VII. In the final determination of the benefits to be provided to the United States of America by the Government of the United Kingdom in return for aid furnished under the Act of Congress of March 11, 1941, the terms and conditions thereof shall be such as not to burden commerce between the two countries, but to promote mutually advantageous economic relations between them and the betterment of worldwide economic relations. To that end, they shall include provision for agreed action by the United States of America and the United Kingdom, open to participation by all other countries of like mind, directed to the expansion, by appropriate international and domestic measures, of production, employment, and the exchange and consumption of goods, which are the material foundations of the liberty and welfare of all peoples; to the elimination of all forms of discriminatory treatment in international commerce, and to the reduction of tariffs and other trade barriers; and, in general, to the attainment of all the economic objectives set forth in the Joint Declaration made on August 12, 1941, by the President of the United States of America and the Prime Minister of the United Kingdom.

"At an early convenient date, conversations shall be begun between the two Governments with a view to determining, in the light of governing economic conditions, the best means of attaining the above-stated objectives by their own agreed action and of seeking the agreed action of other like-minded Governments.

"Article VIII. This Agreement shall take effect as from this day's date. It shall continue in force until a date to be agreed upon by the two Governments.

"Signed and sealed at Washington in duplicate this 23rd day of February, 1942."

No one can yet foresee what the final terms of settlement may be. It seems reasonable, however, to suggest that, whatever the situation may prove to be, it will afford an opportunity to demonstrate again the profound truth of Edmund Burke's plea that "magnanimity in politicks is not seldom the truest wisdom." [10] Burke's plea, in behalf not so much of the American colonists as of the future welfare of the British people themselves, was ignored by a government narrowly intent on asserting what it claimed to be its legal rights. The wheel has come full circle, and it is the British people who must hope that the United States, in pursuance of its own best interests, will follow the path of magnanimity. Narrow calculations, designed on the one side to extract the fullest possible payment and on the other to avoid any but the barest acknowledgment, might well lead to an impasse in which not only would any payment become impossible but hopes for the restoration of mutual prosperity would be doomed to failure.

The best chance, indeed, that substantial payments may be made in the future lies less in a generous im-

[10] Edmund Burke, *Thoughts on the Cause of the Present Discontents* (1770).

mediate settlement than in concentration upon the common task of staving off postwar disintegration and in restoring an expanding system of multilateral trade based upon free exchanges. Negotiations there must be, and in these negotiations each side will naturally and rightly strive to ease the burden on its taxpayers by driving as good a bargain as it can. But the best bargain for both will be possible only if trade is flowing freely again, and no bargain at all may be possible if it is not.[11]

[11] *Cf.* Geoffrey Crowther, *Anglo-American Pitfalls, op. cit.,* pp. 11–12: "In these circumstances, it may be difficult for the British authorities to avoid the retention of some form of exchange control. Moreover, it may have to be exchange control specifically against the dollar; it may be that all other currencies will be plentifully available in London and that only the dollar will be scarce and subject to rationing. Obviously, the dangers of recrimination would then be raised to a maximum . . . circumstances may shape themselves differently. The United States, in its unfailing generosity, may accept recompense for the Lease-Lend goods in some form that does not put a mortgage on the normal flow of British-American trade. The continuance of the gold-buying program may provide an extra source of dollars for the outside world. The tourist traffic may grow to even larger proportions. The level of domestic prosperity in the United States may be so high that American purchases of British goods will be substantially higher than before the war. In general, anything that increases American buying from the sterling area will help to solve the problem. By this means, it might be possible to leave the flow of current trade and services to be settled in a free market, without restrictions, and to confine the exchange control to the movement of capital. If the problem can be reduced to these dimensions, it is certainly soluble, for the American authorities have themselves from time to time called for a curb on the import of 'hot money.' "

The Problem of Reparation

If the handling of intergovernmental obligations between friendly peoples, allied in a common cause, offers such aspects of difficulty, it is obvious that the demand —which will surely be made—that Germany and her aggressive allies should make restitution and reparation will lead also to exceedingly difficult economic and psychological situations. Finland asks reparation from the U.S.S.R. and the U.S.S.R. asks it from Germany; China has suffered heavily in the destruction of her universities, public buildings, and transport; Greece has an account with Italy, and virtually the whole of Europe has been subject to German bombardment, requisitions, and calculated sabotage in the course of establishing the New Order. Hatreds, of intensity unparalleled in the last war, have been created by the ruthlessness of the rule of force. The attempt to establish order by instilling fear will certainly result in the desire to wreak fearful vengeance on the oppressors and all who have co-operated with them. Blood will run in Europe and Asia if and when the hold of the aggressors weakens upon the conquered countries. If for no other reason than to hold these passions in check, co-operation among the United Nations will be the only hope of keeping order during a prolonged transition period.

It is natural enough to feel repulsion at the ruthless

murder of innocent hostages, the cruel and inhuman persecution of minority groups, and the cynical effrontery of the methods by which food and raw materials have been looted and factories stripped or stolen in the guise of bilateral trade. It is equally natural to feel sympathy with the victims of such outrages—with the unfortunate victims of Japanese lust at Nanking and with the bombed households of Chungking as well as with Yugoslav, Czech, Polish, Russian, and other victims of Nazi savagery. From such repulsion and sympathy spring equally natural impulses to exact punishment and revenge upon the actual authors of the outrage, or upon those associated with and condoning their crimes. Detached, cool judgment in these respects is not to be expected from those who have suffered; but the impartial verdict of history, as well as moral teaching and psychological analysis, is overwhelmingly on the side of letting the dead past bury its dead. Peace and prosperity cannot be built on vengeance and hatred, however justified.

Nor can the costs of modern war be met, even after complete victory, by the exaction of tribute. The attempt, in the guise of reparation payments, to make Germany pay after the last war was not successful. It served, however, to bedevil European politics for more than a decade, to provide a rallying point for German resentment, and to negate any possibility of restoring international co-operation. The opinion of economists who have studied this problem is unanimous. Punitive reparations cannot be enforced in the modern world.

Yet there is a real case for insisting not upon punishment, but upon restitution. The democratic powers are even now preparing to make available after the war supplies of foodstuffs and raw materials to the countries that have been overrun and pillaged by the aggressors. Their present poverty is due primarily to the fact that they have been looted systematically by the new trading methods or directly in fulfillment of plans for the New Order. It may be generous and wise for the United Nations to meet the urgent needs of these stricken peoples; but it would also seem both just and sensible to insist that the stolen goods are returned. Moreover, the democratic countries are preparing to take upon themselves the costs of interim policing. Present plans seem to call for relieving Germany, Italy, and Japan of the burden of armaments while retaining that burden on Allied industry. Precautions should be taken against providing German, Italian, and Japanese industry with commercial advantages of this sort. There is a real case for the aggressors' bearing a substantial share of the costs of reconstruction.

As with lease-lend arrangements, this should not "burden commerce" but be used for the "betterment of economic relations." Nor should it provide an occasion for German or Japanese or Italian exports to strengthen their hold of the markets in the conquered countries. The factories that have been torn down or transferred to Germany could well be rebuilt with German labor and materials; Japan could be required to rebuild the Chinese universities that were deliberately attacked. The Danish cattle bought on clearing account, and the blankets and warm clothing requisitioned in many occupied countries for Germany's winter campaign in Russia could be replaced. It would not be unduly difficult to work out a plan by which the German, Italian, and Japanese armament factories could be transferred in large part to the countries they have conquered and despoiled and re-erected under international supervision by the technicians of those countries. The creditors, however, must be willing, as in the case of private debt, to accept payment in goods and services.

Such acts of restitution might well be required at the same time that aid is given to the German, Italian, and Japanese people in meeting immediate necessities and changing over from a war to a peace economy. The frustrated aggressors will inevitably suffer heavily and should pay the price of their misdeeds. The responsible leaders of their populations should pay the price directly in being stripped of their privileges and powers. Many of them will lose their lives. But the victors have a real interest in not permitting whatever governments they may treat with to bear the weight of ostracism and absurd penal tribute. There is a great difference between such ostracism and the requirement that reparation in kind should be made to the victims of the rapacity of the defeated totalitarian governments.

The touchstone of policy, it may be urged, should be

the same as that suggested earlier in connection with the settlement of debts under lease-lend arrangements —namely, how far any given course of action contributes to the establishment of a more stable order and a more co-operative trading system. The economic reversal of totalitarian looting so that the nations that have been strangled and robbed may again be able to live decently, and the satisfaction of their just claims, is obviously to be considered. As will be argued later, international aid in their industrial development is one way in which peaceful trade may be promoted and stabilized.

In the long run, an industrialized central Europe will provide a great market for Germany just as a modernized China might go far to solve Japan's problem of export outlets. When these less-developed areas are strong enough to stand on their feet there is every reason why their great neighbors should be afforded facilities to trade with them; but in the meantime, those neighbors ought not to be allowed to dominate their reconstruction. Indemnities or reparation payments might well give them a chance to do so; restitution of stolen properties need not.

CHAPTER VIII

INTERNATIONAL
ECONOMIC
DEVELOPMENT

New Frontiers of Investment

THERE are three good reasons why, in addition to directing economic policy toward the maintenance of full employment in the great industrial countries, it is important to devise plans of development and modernization in industrially backward areas. These reasons, which are developed in more detail below, may be summarized as the need for new frontiers of investment to occupy the expanded capacity of the great industrial countries, the desirability of raising consumption levels and purchasing power in industrially backward areas, and the necessity of devising new forms of investment to restore a freer flow of international trade.

The first reason derives from the fact that expansionist national economic policies in advanced industrial countries will inevitably encounter a greater demand for consumption goods than for investment goods. The backlog of unfilled demands which is accumulating now is chiefly for commodities of durable, and even immediate, consumption. Automobiles, tires, refrigerators, household appliances, and a wide variety of the lighter manufactures are already in short supply. To build up inventories of such goods, however, it will not be necessary to erect great new factories and equipment, calling for large investment and massive production from the heavy industries, such as iron and steel. The great manufacturing countries are already well supplied with railways and other means of transport, with port facilities, steel-frame factories and offices, and other forms of capital equipment. Replacements and repairs may well be needed, and it is possible that extensive housing programs using prefabricated materials may create new demands for steel; but the bulk of any postwar replacement program must be directed to the lighter manufactures. There has in any case been a marked tendency in this direction.

Upon this tendency, some economists in recent years have developed the so-called "stagnation thesis," to the effect that from time to time savings outrun investment opportunities in a mature economy.[1] What this means simply is that, with the disappearance of the frontier and with population increase tending to slow down, periodic overinvestment cannot be rescued almost auto-

[1] *Cf.* Temporary National Economic Committee, Investigation of Concentration of Economic Power, Hearings, Part 1, Economic Prologue, Part 9, Savings and Investments, pp. 3495-3559 (U. S. Government Printing Office, 1939-40). *See also* A. H. Hansen, *Full Recovery or Stagnation?* (New York, 1938).

matically by fresh surges of expanding demand. In mature economies, mistakes must be written off and adaptations must be made to new circumstances. If the heavy industries are to find adequate markets and new investment outlets are to forestall the cyclical fluctuations of employment arising from disequilibrium between savings and investment, new frontiers must be opened.

Such economic frontiers are to be found for the most part in the provision of equipment for areas that still lack modern industrial facilities, such for example as central and eastern Europe, China, Latin America, and in many respects the U.S.S.R. That unfulfilled demands for capital equipment exist on a great scale may easily be demonstrated.[2] Pressure on the Soviet railway system, even before the war, as measured by the ton-miles carried per linear mile of railroad, was heavier than in any other country. China's railways are in utter disrepair and confusion. The traffic along the difficult Burma road is eloquent evidence of the possibilities that await the construction of transport facilities through the densely populated river valleys. Latin America lacks air transport and basic heavy industries. The whole of central and eastern Europe is underequipped in these respects.

The problem confronting the developed industrial

[2] Cf. Oscar R. Hobson, *The Function of Foreign Lending*, International Chamber of Commerce, Berlin Congress (1937), Document No. 3.

countries will certainly be aggravated by the tapering off of armament programs when the war ends. Coal, steel, aluminum, heavy machinery, machine tools, aircraft, trucks, and tanks will no longer be needed in such vast quantities; but the equipment for producing them will be greatly in excess of civilian demands unless new outlets can be found for the products of heavy industry.

Raising Consumption Levels

The second reason for planning international economic development is that only by the provision of modern facilities for transport and production will it be possible to increase the national incomes of the industrially backward areas, and so raise consumption levels to the point where their domestic economic problems may become manageable, and both their importing demands and their capacity to pay for imports will be increased.

"The destruction of the poor is their poverty." Nations as well as individuals may get into a situation where they are too poor to command, or even to desire, the means to raise themselves out of their poverty and inefficiency. The most baffling economic problem faced by countries with low living standards is not so much their poverty as their inefficiency and lack of initiative.[3] Inadequate nutrition and endemic disease

[3] Cf. R. K. Das, *The Industrial Efficiency of India* (London, 1930).

sap the vitality of great masses of the world's population.[4] Lack of capital inhibits the construction of
public-health facilities, of transport and productive
mechanisms that would enhance the value of their labor,
of educational systems that would improve efficiency.
The impoverished countries become caught in an in-
exorable cycle of population increase pressing constantly upon the limits of subsistence.

To break through that cycle demands new stimulus
from outside. Even though the first lifting of subsistence limits and control of disease result in increased
survival, it is only by increasing production faster than
population that a surplus of resources may be secured
with which to achieve the beginnings of educational
and economic progress. The experience of Europe in
the nineteenth century was that population grew, but
production grew faster; and as production grew it
changed social conditions so that higher living standards were sought, and ultimately the Western world
achieved control of its own natural increase. England
trod this path first; but the whole Western world followed close on its heels. After 1868, Japan broke from
its economic medievalism in precisely the same way.

In our own day, Soviet Russia has demonstrated that
in one generation a country can go far on the road of
industrial development. Before 1914, despite the intro-

[4] *Cf.* League of Nations, European Conference on Rural Life,
Geneva, 1939. League of Nations, Health Organization, Intergov-
ernmental Conference of Far Eastern Countries on Rural Hygiene,
Geneva, 1937.

duction of some industries, only 17.7 per cent of Russia's population were urban industrial workers. A quarter of a century later, the proportion was 32.8 per cent.[5] Revolution, civil war, and famines had ravaged the U.S.S.R. in those years, and little capital had come from the outside world; but productivity had been improved and there was some rise in consumption levels even though most of the increased productivity went into the fashioning of a great mechanized army and its supporting industries. Perhaps most important of all, the traditional peasant outlook had been transformed.

This lesson will not be lost upon the industrially backward peoples, especially those who live in Slavic Europe and in Asia. It may be that the last opportunity, not only to develop the economic resources of these areas as part of a great world trading system, but also to restore co-operative relations between the U.S.S.R. and the Western democracies, will be presented at the close of this war. The need of the industrially backward countries is great. The prospects of reorganizing stable governments and improving the productivity and consumption levels of great masses of people are paralleled by the possibility of initiating democratic procedures in areas that are not yet ready for the full exercise of democratic responsibilities.

The conjuncture of overcapacity in the industrial

---

[5] *Quarterly Bulletin of Soviet-Russian Economics* (edited by Professor S. N. Prokopovicz), No. 4 (Geneva, April, 1940), p. 1.

countries and industrial needs in the backward countries offered an opportunity after the last war. The great leader of the Chinese Revolution, Dr. Sun Yat-sen, in a book that has received too little attention, offered the needs of China as a solution for the industrial problems of the West.[6] His ideas attracted a good deal of attention, but there was a real scarcity of capital, and at that time the problems nearer home were urgent. Like many another prophet also, Sun Yat-sen was despised and rejected by the experts. The practical suggestions of his book were not prepared by technicians and were not very convincing. Its fundamental thesis remains sound.

New Forms of Investment

The third reason why projects of international economic development deserve serious attention at the present time is to be found in the fact that the methods of capitalist enterprise by which the Industrial Revolution spread to undeveloped countries in the nineteenth century are no longer effective. The railways of Europe, of the British Dominions, of South America, and in some measure those of the United States also, were built with the aid of British capital and largely by British enterprise. British shipping crossed the seven

[6] Sun Yat-sen, *The International Development of China* (New York and London, 1922).

seas. Capital, in Bagehot's phrase, "ran everywhere as it was wanted or as the rate of interest tempted it." Refrigerating works in Argentina, oil fields in Mexico, Iran, and a score of other countries, tin mines in Malaya, copper in the Belgian Congo were developed by private enterprise.

But the same combination of social controls and economic nationalism that was noted in discussing national economic policies has hampered international enterprise more and more. The lack of political stability after 1918, and finally the breakdown of exchange equilibrium in 1931, completed the process. The flow of venture capital, which had dwindled even before 1931, dried up almost completely thereafter and was replaced by the erratic movements of "hot money" seeking, not profit, but refuge and security. The security sought was from depreciation, and the seeking of security ensured depreciation.

If evidence were needed of the difficulties confronting the use of private capital in modernizing the equipment of industrially backward areas, it might be found in the history of the banking consortium organized after 1918 to proffer financial aid to China.[7] The problem was primarily political. China was afraid of losing its political independence if it opened the door to a struggle of rival imperialisms. The foreign investors were afraid that political instability in China would endanger

[7] *Cf.* Frederick V. Field, *American Participation in the Chinese Consortiums* (Chicago, 1931).

their investments. The consortium, created with the approval of President Wilson in 1920, represented very powerful banking interests in France, Japan, and Great Britain, as well as in the United States.[8] It had powerful diplomatic support from the governments of these four countries; but despite China's urgent desire for capital and the consortium's willingness to consider any reasonable terms for new loans, the Chinese Government never ceased to oppose it. The reason clearly reflected "not so much objection to the specific terms of that plan as their mistrust of any foreign organization formed ostensibly for China's benefit." [9] Like other and later committees for financial assistance to debtor countries, the consortium not unnaturally drifted into the position of a creditor group endeavoring to safeguard past investment. Since 1929 it has not shown any sign of life.

Yet there are solid reasons for believing that China and other industrially backward areas have less to fear from private foreign investment than from government lending, which is apt to be spasmodic and is seldom free of political, as distinct from economic, motives. China's experience with the so-called Nishihara loans, negotiated by Japanese agents with corrupt war lords in a period of political instability, has been productive of more grief than any of the private loans for such

[8] *Cf. ibid.*, pp. 165–66 for a list of the member banks in each country.
[9] *Ibid.*, p. 189.

productive investments as railroad construction. The first essential is clearly that China shall be strong, united, and free. Her record as a debtor to Chinese banks is good. There would seem to be no reason why a strong and unified China should not afford attractive opportunities for venture capital, nor why such capital, divorced from political support, should endanger China's political independence. The model of the loans floated under League of Nations auspices for the reconstruction of Austria is worth considering in this connection. Such loans, subscribed by private investors in a comprehensive international arrangement, are less likely to impair national sovereignty than loans advanced by individual governments for political reasons or short-term banking accommodation which is liable to be withdrawn suddenly in a crisis.[10]

The experience of many private enterprises with the government agencies of the U.S.S.R. goes to show that the collaboration of private enterprise is not wholly impossible even with revolutionary governments, provided the latter are strong enough to give and discharge reasonable guarantees over a short period. There will undoubtedly be a place for such collaboration in providing commercial credits and certain forms of investment capital. This collaboration may at times reach considerable proportions, wherever governments in need of capital and technical assistance are strong

[10] *Cf.* Helmut G. Callis, *Foreign Capital in Southeast Asia* (New York, 1942); especially the introduction by Professor Carl F. Remer.

enough to give assurances of political stability and economic returns. It is not in regard to such governments that international development projects may prove necessary. It may be possible, for example, that reorganization of industrial equipment in the U.S.S.R. and great capital investments in central Europe, as well as in China and Latin America, may be negotiable by firmly established governments with private enterprises in the United States.

It is to be noted, however, that negotiations for such private investment in the development of iron and steel production utilizing the rich ores of Brazil were finally taken over by an agency of the United States Government.[11] The probabilities are that material assistance in kind or technical services, patterned either upon lease-lend procedures or upon the short-term credit recently opened by the United States in favor of the U.S.S.R., will prove more important in the immediate postwar period than private lending. It is possible, indeed, to conceive of an International Investment Authority through which development projects may be financed.

Mistakes after World War I

Such private lending as does occur ought not to follow the pattern and repeat the mistakes of the ill-advised loan flow to Europe between 1925 and 1929.

[11] The *New York Times* (September 27, 29, 1940).

These loans were ruinous to those who subscribed to them. Expert opinion is unanimous, also, that although the loans no doubt contributed to the development of the borrowing countries, the character of the lending —too much on short-term and excessive amounts lent in the later nineteen twenties—created a serious transfer problem to which too little attention was paid. An international consultative agency should be created to supervise both the amount and the character of the loans to be negotiated.

The stream of credit that flowed to Europe after the first sound loans had restored prosperity supported for a few years an economic situation that was inherently unstable because the later loans were excessive in the aggregate and too many of them were on short-term. The credit of the borrowing countries collapsed when the loan stream was stopped at its source.

Not public loans, but direct investments, self-liquidating within a reasonably short period, would seem a preferable form of private capital investment for reconstruction. Even the soundest of such investments, however, cannot survive a period of economic nationalism and political instability such as afflicted Europe in the years between the wars. Capital will move productively again between the nations only if peace can be assured and if trade flows freely. Private foreign investment cannot be the beginning, though it may be a desirable consequence, of political and economic reorganization after the war.

The experience of the League of Nations is illuminating in this regard. Its achievements were considerable. Those achievements have often been misunderstood because of the great publicity that was given to the financial aspects of the international assistance to Austria and Hungary. A remarkable example of what is possible by the provision of technical aid and organization, with modest financial support, is provided by the work done in connection with the resettlement of Greek refugees from Asia Minor. An account of this work by an American who himself brought remarkable qualities to the task is worth reading at the present time.[12]

The moral encouragement and authority of assistance from the outside world, personified by disinterested experts of high character and courage, is perhaps the greatest aid that can be given to stricken and bewildered communities. This moral quality of the League reconstruction work in Austria and Hungary was as important as the technical skill and financial aid necessary to carry through a comprehensive scheme of reconstruction. Relief on a piecemeal scale was not adequate to the situation. Both technical skill and financial assistance were needed, but neither would have been of much avail if the communities concerned had not rallied with confidence around the leadership provided by the League representatives. It was a remark-

[12] Charles P. Howland, *Greek Refugee Settlement*, Geneva, 1926 (II, Economic and Financial, 1926.II.32).

able demonstration of solidarity among the representatives of the world community, and this was perhaps the secret of immediate success in the early stages of reconstruction. Inflationary panic ceased, confidence returned, and the community went back to work.

The reconstruction loans were an essential element of the comprehensive reorganization that was achieved. They were floated with every possible guarantee by the co-operating governments and administered with scrupulous care. No financial skill, however, could have availed against the disasters which overtook the reconstruction projects in the great depression and the subsequent political upheavals.

The League loans ultimately failed of their purpose, but their failure was a casualty of the general European disintegration—not of any flaw in their negotiation. Their security was undermined by excessive lending at a later stage without sufficient concern for the problem of transfer. The ultimate problem that was not solved, however, was the problem of political security. Without that, the most carefully negotiated financial security is an illusion.

The Importance of Technical Aid

The promising beginnings of technical collaboration between experts selected by the League and the national government of China offer another illustration of what may be done even without great financial loans. Expert members of the League secretariat, and other experts recommended by the Council and employed by the Chinese Government, did yeoman work in reorganizing or creating public-health services, surveying engineering problems, planning river conservation and afforestation, advising on civil-service organization, agricultural co-operation, flood relief, and many other technical problems.[13] The number and variety of technical services thus made available to the Chinese Government are not generally realized. In addition to the foreign technicians who went to work as servants of the Chinese Government, a stream of Chinese technicians came to consult and study American and European methods in their particular fields and were advised in their studies by competent members of the League secretariat.

This point has been stressed because it is essential to emphasize the fact that capital is not the sole or even the main need of undeveloped industrial countries. Their primary need is skilled administrators and technicians; and this is ultimately a problem of training a greater number of organizers and experts among their own people. Foreign assistance and advice, if it is disinterested and placed at the disposal of the national community concerned, rather than of some private

[13] *Cf.* League of Nations Committee on Technical Co-operation between the League of Nations and China, *Report of the Technical Agent of the Council on His Mission in China* (Geneva, 1934).

enterprise or foreign power, can be of considerable service, especially when they provide visible evidence of understanding, sympathy, and help from the outside world. Such disinterested service rapidly acquires prestige and authority which is often quite out of proportion to the authority of the persons concerned in their own countries.

International assistance to countries in need of help after this war must probably develop first out of the administrative machinery devised to handle the interim problems of the transition period. Engineers, medical men, scientists, economists, and administrative experts, working from the assured bases of international collaboration projected in the reprovisioning plans of the Inter-Allied Agreement signed at London on September 24, 1941, might well administer those plans in such a way as to lead to wider forms of collaboration after the immediate emergency is past. Such forms of collaboration in the reconstruction of economic activity should be directed primarily to higher consumption levels and to the stabilizing and consolidation of the new governments along democratic lines. It may well be that for the achievement of these aims foreign capital will be needed, perhaps in large amounts; but the first essential is organization. It is worth-while to think now, not in terms of international charity after the war, but in terms of mutual assistance to increase productivity, to raise consumption levels, and to restore the free flow of mutually beneficial trade. Investment in

the vitality and efficiency of the working population
should begin at home, but it should not stop there. It
will pay greater dividends than any extractive enterprise.

Refugee Settlement

There is a particular aspect of international economic development in which far-reaching plans have
already been laid. The address of Mr. Sumner Welles
to the Inter-American Jewish Conference at Baltimore
on November 23, 1941, traced the organization of intergovernmental plans for refugee settlement from the
Evian Conference of July, 1938.[14] The desperate plight
of millions of unfortunate opponents or victims of totalitarian persecution surpasses in horror any story of
medieval or oriental cruelty. Nor is this wholly a Jewish problem by any means.

The modern refugee problem begins with the Russian Revolution in 1917. Besides the numerous colonies
of emigrés in such centers of refuge as Paris, there have
been, and still are, large numbers of "white" Russians
in the most desperate straits in the Far East, particularly Harbin and Shanghai. The outbreak of war in
the Pacific has added new problems in that region. As
racial and political hatreds grew in intensity during
the interwar years, successive groups of Social Demo-

[14] Cf. *New York Times* (November 24, 1941), p. 5.

crats and other opponents of militarist despotism were driven from their homelands. Hundreds of thousands were driven from Spain, and many of them remain in concentration camps in France. Their numbers were increased by refugees from Austria, Czechoslovakia, and finally from all European countries that came under the Nazi heel.[15]

The total number of expatriate refugees now runs into the millions. There are substantial numbers of Jews among them, but they are by no means a majority. The problems presented by their absorption, or even by their temporary accommodation, are very difficult of solution. Private charitable groups, particularly Jewish committees who have not confined their help to their own people, have done remarkable work in placing and sustaining individuals; but the scope of the problem exceeds the resources of any private action that may be conceived. Every possible exit from persecution is choked with refugees unable to get farther. Lisbon is a case in point. Desperate groups have roamed the seas in leaky ships, unable to gain entry to any country. Shanghai, already crowded with escapees, has received a new influx of homeless and often penniless wanderers. The more hospitable of the Latin American Republics, such as Cuba, have more refugees for per-

[15] Cf. Sir John Hope-Simpson, *The Refugee Problem: Report of a Survey* (London, 1939); and *Refugees: A Review of the Situation since September, 1938* (London, 1939). In addition to these sources, use has been made of an unpublished MS prepared for the author by Mr. Joseph Conard.

manent settlement or in transit than they can handle. Central China has millions of refugees from the areas in Japanese occupation.

These millions escaped the imminent risk of execution, but many of them in so doing abandoned all their possessions. No more can do so at present. Even if shipping were available, every country now imposes severe conditions of entry. The fear of "fifth-column activity" complicates the situation in strategic areas. There is, therefore, a virtually complete stoppage of refugee migration.

The millions among the persecuted minority groups who are left at the mercy of ruthless tyrannies are in process of extermination. They are deported to bleak and unprepared areas in pursuance of grandiose schemes of population redistribution; they are subjected to discrimination in the distribution of food, to confiscation of capital, to exclusion from employment; the sexes are often separated; there are wholesale mass executions. By all these methods a systematic campaign of extinction is being waged against them with a cold-blooded and premeditated cruelty that many people in more fortunate countries cannot conceive and therefore too often dismiss as exaggerated antitotalitarian propaganda. The evidence, unfortunately, is undeniable; indeed, those in charge of totalitarian policy do not deny but justify and defend their actions.[16]

[16] Cf. Speech by Dr. Goebbels quoted in *Time* (November 24, 1941), p. 31.

It is obvious that totalitarian oppression has in the past counted upon the humanitarianism of the democratic countries to welcome and care for its victims. There have been occasions, in fact, when cynical attempts have been made to make profit out of the situation. The refugees, by legal and illegal means, have been systematically stripped of their possessions; but in addition the Nazi government had the effrontery to offer a plan whereby permission for mass migration of Jews might be purchased by the payment of large sums in dollars for their travel expenses! There is no possible solution of the refugee problem if the democratic countries accept without protest the responsibility of caring for all the opponents of totalitarianism and for anyone else the tyrannical governments wish to drive out for racial or other reasons. The only real solution is to stop the persecution and pillage of minorities. The only way in which to do this is to defeat and destroy the cruel and unscrupulous tyrannies that have created this problem.

Even when this has been done, there will be a tremendous problem of resettlement. Some of the political exiles will undoubtedly return to their homelands. Indeed, the governments at present in exile must count upon the repatriation of many of their citizens. This will doubtless be taken care of by the intergovernmental bureau to which reference has been made above.[17] Most of the exiled governments and many of

[17] Cf. page 53.

the individual exiles have blocked funds in considerable amounts which may be repatriated after the war.

There will remain, however, hundreds of thousands of refugees to be taken care of, and for most of them repatriation would be undesirable and undesired. They must find new homes and new opportunities. It was to grapple with this problem that the President of the United States convened an Intergovernmental Committee at Evian in July, 1938. This Committee created a continuing organization and appointed a permanent secretariat. The International Labor Organization also has a Migration Commission, and the League of Nations has its Minority Section. In addition, there are powerful private agencies at work and the President's Advisory Committee has, with their aid, made surveys of possible settlement areas. One such experimental settlement, at Sosua in Santo Domingo, is already in operation. But after the war the problem will demand action on a much greater scale and by varying methods. If political difficulties can be adjusted, the Jewish reconstruction of Palestine, which can count upon a large and steady import of capital, may absorb large numbers of refugees. Mexico has opened her doors to Spanish refugees, and other Latin American countries may welcome reinforcement of their populations, especially if capital comes with the immigrants.

Infiltration into already settled communities, if wisely controlled, is in many respects preferable to group settlements in difficult areas of uncertain resources. Such infiltration, however, depends upon careful selection and training of the prospective immigrants. It depends also upon a co-operative attitude in the receiving countries which will be difficult to secure unless those countries share after the war in expanding world trade and prosperity. Certain promising projects of group settlement—in Kenya and the Philippines, for example—could be brought into operation also.

As in so many other of these problems, the practical obstacle is not lack of expert knowledge or practical plans, but the difficulty of securing political agreement among conflicting interests. The only way in which this difficulty can be resolved is by organizing effective international machinery whose driving force derives from the continuing interest of the great democratic governments in assuring its success.

CHAPTER IX

THE DILEMMA OF
COMMERCIAL POLICY

Access to Raw Materials

THE cautious wording and reservations of the fourth point of the Atlantic Charter are significant of the difficulties that confront any attempt to envisage the restoration of a freer trading system.[1] It is not possible to interpret this statement precisely in terms of practical policies. Article VII of the Anglo-American Mutual Aid agreement, signed on February 23, 1942, is somewhat less qualified in its statements regarding tariffs and trade barriers; but its language is still very general.[2]

There is obviously a growing recognition of the fact, for fact it is, that the improvement of living standards or even their maintenance depends in large measure upon access in some fashion to raw materials scattered about the globe. For the first time in its history, the United States is being made aware of the de-

---

[1] *Cf.* text quoted on p. 64 of this book.
[2] *Cf.* text quoted on p. 159 of this book.

pendence of its industries upon imported raw materials. Germany, Italy, and Japan must use every possible means to replenish their stocks of alloy minerals, if not by running the blockade, then by use of the commercial air lines. The use of reserve stocks, scrap, substitute materials, and civilian supplies must be supplemented by looting the conquered peoples; and even then there is a steady dwindling of available resources. The prewar slogan, "we must export or die," has become, in Dr. Goebbels' recent broadcasts, "we must conquer or die." Unless access can be gained to sources of oil, rubber, textiles, and alloy minerals, the vast industrial production necessary for modern war must ultimately be curtailed. The limits of civilian consumption may be compressed, ingenious substitutes may be devised, and waste material may be reclaimed in greater measure than most experts had believed possible; but the costs run high, and there are limits to the efficiency of such makeshifts. Though real gains may be made in the application of new scientific processes, they do not compensate in the aggregate for the lack of access to abundant natural raw materials.

It is sometimes argued, and with some justice, that the progress of applied science has made possible a high degree of economic self-sufficiency in the most advanced industrial countries.[3] The extent to which

[3] *Cf.* Lancelot Hogben, "Planning for Human Survival," in *What Is Ahead of Us?* (London, 1937), pp. 188–89: "We are now on the threshold of an age of hydro-electric power, of electrolytic chemical processes, of light metals which exist in abundance everywhere.

this is true, however, can easily be exaggerated, and against it must be set the fact that the most modern forms of scientific production often call for the widest collection of dispersed raw materials—copper, tin, rubber, vanadium, tungsten, and a long list of others. There does not seem much reason to believe that in our time the problem of access to these materials will cease to be an important consideration in shaping national economic policies. The obvious way to provide access is by restoring international trade. If this cannot be done, a stupendous economic disaster must ensue for great masses of workers in the raw-material-producing countries.

This problem of access to raw materials was not serious as long as trade flowed freely. But such a statement masks the difficult realities of the present situation. Trade, and with it capital, flowed freely as long as it was not a prime instrument of national policy. The nineteenth-century trading world, which witnessed such vast changes in economic relationships, was centered on the London money market. Britain's naval power was undisputed, and her industrial leadership

---

Cellulose is beginning to displace coal as a source of synthetic operations. Fertilizers, tank-culture, and applied genetics have made land the least important part of capital equipment in food production. Civil aviation, the light car, television, and broadcasting provide an escape from the disadvantages of cultural isolation contingent on small community life. Urban congestion is unnecessary. A much higher potential of self-sufficiency exists, and the advent of a light metal economy will remove one of the principal sources of national rivalries."

was not seriously challenged till toward the end of the nineteenth century. Her merchants and investors grew rich by reason of the development of world trade. It was they, more than any statesman, who "called a new world into existence to redress the balance of the old." Britain did not need to regulate foreign investment and direct the flow of trade in order to buttress her world power. That power was enhanced by allowing trade and capital to flow freely.

The free-trade argument of the classical economists was based upon these conditions. In the course of time the element of naval power in the background came to be ignored or forgotten, and commercial policy was directed toward the creation of equal trading opportunities for private enterprise in every market. The main instruments of commercial policy were the "treaties of commerce and navigation" assuring both "national treatment" and "most-favored-nation treatment." The first endeavored to secure for the foreign trader the same status and rights as were enjoyed by national citizens of the country where he was trading. The second was a promise that preferential treatment would not be given to the traders of any third country. It is still one of the cornerstones of United States policy and is now usually referred to as "equality of trading opportunity." In colonial or semicolonial areas it becomes the principle of "the open door," which has been championed by the United States ever since John Hay enunciated it in those terms.

The Spread of Economic Nationalism

This attempt to break down the barriers to trade between local areas in newly constituted nation-states and to diminish the barriers to trade between those states received its first severe check when Continental Europe refused to adapt its agriculture to the flood of cheap grain from the New World and when, at the same time, the new countries insisted on protecting their manufacturing industries. The great bilateral treaty negotiated by Cobden and Chevalier in 1860 had promised to open an era of progressively freer trade; but the increase in the American protective tariffs after the Civil War, the French reversal of policy after 1870, and Germany's adoption in 1879 of high protection based on "the compact of iron and rye" put an entirely different complexion on commercial policies. The age of plenty was hardly launched before the element of power politics was again introduced. There was a steady development thenceforward of economic nationalism, which has now reached its ultimate expression in the totalitarian state.[4]

---

[4] Cf. A. J. Toynbee, *A Study of History*, Vol. IV, p. 175: "Economic nationalism may be defined as an exploitation of the apparatus of a parochial state for the purpose of promoting the economic interests of the population of that state at the expense of the rest of Mankind. On the moral plane such a policy is indefensible in any circumstances; and in an industrialized world it is also economically disastrous for all parties, since it is attempting the

Every nation-state has now adopted in some measure
the apparatus of mercantilism. This is inevitable in a
period of "total war." Even the United States has been
forced to adopt such measures of economic warfare
as blocked accounts, preclusive buying, export control, and import quotas. Great Britain, the nineteenth-
century protagonist of free trade, is using the whole
armory of economic warfare. Financial transfers the
world over are subject to exchange control. Commodity trade is no longer conducted on a competitive,
multilateral basis, but is convoyed along bilateral channels selected for strategic reasons. National production
is commandeered at fixed prices and bartered in bulk.

---

impossible in trying to harness the intrinsically oecumenical force
of Industrialism to a parochial aim. At the same time it is manifest
in retrospect that an epidemic of Economic Nationalism was the
inevitable nemesis of letting this new oecumenical force of Industrialism loose in a world in which parochial states were the
reigning political institution. For a community which keys up its
economic life to the tension and the rhythm of Industrialism is
consciously or unconsciously setting itself the ambition of making
its country into a 'Workship of the World'; and as one local community after another undergoes the Industrial Revolution there is
bound to be a competition between a number of local industrial
Powers for the same world-market. Owing to the frailty of human
nature, such competition usually provokes conflict before it pro-
motes cooperation; the conflict tempts the combatants to resort
to whatever weapons may come to hand; and a whole armoury of
weapons for an economic conflict between local industrial Powers
is offered, ready-made, in the apparatus for economic warfare
which the parochial states of our latter-day Western World have inherited from the age of 'Mercantilism,' when privileged commercial oligarchies were joining in 'the sport of kings' by using states
as instruments for capturing from one another the international
trade in superfluities."

The Australian report previously quoted puts the situation very simply when it says:

"Within a few months of the outbreak of the war the Government had organised the whole of the export trade of Australia and placed it under the control of Boards and Commissions acting on behalf of the Government. In wool, wheat, butter, metals and fruit representing over £100 million of exports, the whole of the commercial interests normally engaged in the export trade have become agents for the Government working on a commission basis."

Can anyone expect that, after the war ends, such controls will suddenly disappear? The bitter experience of totalitarian war—prepared over long years by methods in which the subordination of plenty to power in the conduct of commercial policies was an essential element—will not easily be forgotten. Totalitarian autarky would have failed of its purpose if it had not been able to draw strength from the disunity of the countries which clung to relatively free trading systems operated by private enterprise.[5] It was in fact parasitic upon the free-trading world and never hesitated to make raids upon the resources of that world whenever opportunity offered.

A clear example of the way in which an unscrupulous financial and trading policy could raid the resources of other countries as long as it had access to a free-exchange market was provided by the manner

[5] *Cf.* Douglas Miller, *op. cit.*, ch. 2.

in which Japanese banks, operating in the free-exchange market of Shanghai, secured control of large amounts of foreign exchange lent by the United States and British Governments to support the Chinese yuan in the early stages of the war between that currency and the Japanese puppet currencies. The foreign-exchange assets were put at the disposal of British and Chinese banks in Shanghai to defend the exchange parity of the yuan. Using Chinese currency, taken apparently from the Chinese Maritime Customs funds collected in Japanese-controlled ports and lodged in Japanese banks, a bear attack was launched on the yuan. To avoid a break in the exchange, the Chinese agencies bought the offered yuan, and their foreign-exchange reserves thus passed into the hands of the Japanese. When support was withdrawn from the yuan, its exchange value broke and the Japanese could repurchase cheaply and replace the relatively small amounts of yuan they had sold to start the speculative attack. Such an operation could not be repeated since support for the Chinese currency was later given through bilaterally controlled exchange operations and an import licensing system which was, until war broke out, centered at Hong Kong. This arrangement, however, entailed a short-circuiting of the Shanghai free market, where the yuan was worth around 2½ cents as compared with its controlled rate of $5^{11}\!/_{32}$ cents at Hong Kong.

As long as totalitarian trading policies have access

to a free market, raids of this character will always be possible. Therefore, it seems inevitable that whatever trading arrangements exist between the countries endeavoring to restore multilateral commodity trade and free multilateral exchange operations, they must protect themselves against the operations of countries which do not co-operate with them.

There is much to be said, however, for a generous economic peace combined with strict political and even military conditions. The totalitarian countries must be taught that war does not pay, but peace does. After their defeat, their industrial power will prove to have been weakened by their concentration upon war preparation and above all by their repression of free education and research. Provided that severe political control prohibits them from following once more methods of economic preparation for renewed warfare, the risks of freer trade will not be great.

Transitional Controls

For the interim period, which should not be prolonged beyond what is necessary, it would seem probable that present arrangements (including the commandeering of agricultural and raw-material export surpluses at fixed prices and their sale in bulk by bilateral purchase agreements, together with exchange control operated by consultative agreement) must be continued and gradually liberalized so as to give greater flexibility and adaptation to individual consumer demands. The experience of Austria in the years 1934–36 proves that the regulation of commodity trade and exchange transfers can be diminished by progressively liberal administration within the framework of severe controls.[6] Those countries which are successful in emancipating themselves quickly from war controls will gain a great trading advantage.

It is by no means sure, however, that such mitigation of regulated and directed trade will be accepted as a goal toward which to work, as political conditions are stabilized and peacetime production is restored. Some authorities are impressed by the desirability of retaining public control over the exchanges, if only in order to allow the unhampered operation of expansionist monetary policies. Few economists are now willing to advocate "flexible" exchanges, though most of them agree that, in a crisis, adjustment of the exchange rate is preferable to a violent policy of price deflation.[7] Those who still inveigh against the tyranny of stable exchange rates in effect

[6] Cf. J. B. Condliffe, *The Reconstruction of World Trade* (New York, 1941), pp. 244–45; and Howard S. Ellis, *Exchange Control in Central Europe* (Cambridge, Mass., 1941); especially ch. 2, "Austrian Exchange Control: an Example of Successful Termination."

[7] Cf. Sir Alfred Davidson, *The Economics of Peace* (Sydney, 1941), pp. 31–6.

refuse to accept the necessity for adjusting the national economies to changes in international equilibrium. There are some also who visualize exchange
control as a potent means of reorienting national production along socialist lines. Others again seek in a
"mixed system" some compromise between laissez
faire and totalitarian regimentation.[8] The pressure
upon practical politicians to depreciate or control the
exchange rate in order to protect vested interests
threatened by competition will be very heavy.

The difficulty about all these proposals to continue
exchange control is well stated by Professor Howard
S. Ellis in his detailed, technical analysis of exchange
control in Europe.

"Sooner or later virtually every exchange-control system
has lost its original orientation toward the monetary
standard and capital flight and has become an instrument
for ulterior ends." [9]

British and American Policy

Official United States policy, as repeatedly declared
by the Secretary of State, Mr. Cordell Hull, and recently restated emphatically by the Under Secretary

[8] Cf. Eugene Staley, *World Economy in Transition* (New York,
1939), Part III, "Laissez Faire and Planning," and Part V, "Problems of Policy in a Mixed System," especially pp. 234–45.

[9] Howard S. Ellis, *op. cit.*, p. 297.

of State,[10] remains fixed upon the restoration of multilateral, free exchange.

"The cornerstone and basis of America's foreign trade policy is the principle of equality of treatment. The American system rests upon the premise that multilateral trade and payments, facilitated by the principle of equality of treatment and originating in private enterprise and initiative, provide the system most calculated to expand the world's real income and so improve the real standard of living of the peoples of the world." [11]

The wording of the fourth point of the Atlantic Charter, promising to "further the enjoyment by all states, great or small, victor or vanquished, of access, on equal terms, to the trade and to the raw materials of the world," reflects the official United States view —which was also official British policy for long decades before the Chamberlain regime of protection and of preference within the British Commonwealth and Empire.

The crux of decisions in respect of international trade, in the transitional period after the war during which emergency controls must be maintained, will almost certainly be reached in negotiations between Britain and the United States. The international economic situation of Great Britain is certain to be seriously weakened after the war. Its foreign earning

[10] Speech of Under Secretary of State Sumner Welles at the World Trade Dinner of the National Foreign Trade Convention, *New York Times* (October 8, 1941), p. 14.
[11] Henry J. Tasca, *World Trading Systems* (Paris, 1939), p. 141.

assets have been seriously depleted. The temptation to drive bilateral trade bargains is likely to be great and to be backed by pressure from domestic interests,[12] since by such bargains exports may be promoted to secure the great volume of imports needed by a country so highly industrialized and densely populated.

Unless an expanding system of multilateral trade can be quickly restored, Great Britain may be tempted to entrench itself in an imperial system of exchange control supplemented by imperial preference and bilateral barter treaties with countries in its trading area. It is to be hoped that Britain will not yield to this temptation, since, if it does, the chances of restoring multilateral trade and free exchanges are remote, and the United States may then be tempted to make the best bargains it can along similar lines. The United States is badly placed to do so with its high tariff, export surpluses of both agricultural and manufactured products, and its strong creditor position. Great Britain, with its far-flung interests and heavy overhead, would be well advised also to think twice before jeopardizing its international trading position by enclosing itself in the strait-jacket of bilateral barter agreements and exchange control.

The best interests of both the United States and

[12] Examples of such pressure may be cited from the House of Commons debates on postwar agriculture as reported in the *Economist* (November 29, 1941). *Cf. also* the correspondence to which this report gave rise, *Economist* (December 13, 1941).

Great Britain, as well as the only hope of restoring an expanding system of multilateral trade, lie in joint effort to restrain an inflationary boom followed by deflationary panic. Only by concerted effort to avoid violent price fluctuations while carrying through necessary adjustments to the new postwar situation can full employment be maintained. The national economic policy of the United States is crucial in this respect. If production, employment, and prices can be sustained in the United States, the demands of its industry for raw materials and of its consumers for imported manufactures will go far to sustain production, employment, and prices in other countries.

Given such a situation it should not prove impossible, after the first shocks of transition have been withstood and democratic order has been restored in Europe, to negotiate adjustments of international economic relations that will lead ultimately to a more stable equilibrium. One element in such negotiations must be the finding of a workable exchange relationship between the dollar and sterling.[13] There is some tendency in Great Britain to minimize the efficiency of sterling depreciation as a means of righting the balance of payments.[14] In some measure, this tendency

[13] *Cf.* Seymour E. Harris, *op. cit.*, ch. 13, for a discussion of the possibility of appreciating the dollar by lowering the buying price of gold.

[14] *Cf.* Geoffrey Crowther, *Anglo-American Pitfalls, op. cit.*, also "Post-War Economic Problems II" in *Bulletin of International News* (London, April 4, 1942), pp. 276–83.

seems to flow from the war experience of exchange control maximizing the foreign-exchange receipts for exports in strong demand. It is true that many important British exports sell freely in the United States when prices are high; but this does not mean that high prices are the cause of the demand for these products or that more would not sell if their dollar prices could be lowered by a depreciation of sterling without interfering with industrial recovery in the United States. The cause both of the strong demand and of the high prices is the maintenance of purchasing power in the United States. Moreover, British colonial exports provide appreciable amounts of dollar exchange as Britain's exports to neutral markets do indirectly. The case for depreciation rests on wider bases than direct Anglo-American trade. One would imagine that the disastrous consequences of the opposite policy after the last war, when sterling became overvalued from 1925 onward, would be convincing evidence of the desirability of finding a dollar rate for sterling compatible with the relative levels of costs and prices (including wage rates) in the United States and Great Britain.[15] It is too soon yet to calculate whether such a rate would involve a depreciation of sterling from its present level. Costs in the United States, and especially labor costs, are high and tend to rise.

[15] For the consequences of the 1925 blunder, *cf.* J. Maynard Keynes, *The Economic Consequences of Sterling Parity* (New York, 1925).

The time at which provisional stabilization of the dollar-sterling rate might be attempted, and the proper level of stabilization, could be decided only by the experts charged with the operation of the exchange stabilization funds. British and American authorities would obviously have to agree on the new rate and protect it by joint action against speculative capital movements. If the rate were well chosen, such speculative movements would be minimized. If it were soundly based upon a restoration of equilibrium in the price-cost structure of each national economy, it would be relatively easy to maintain.

Reduction of tariffs and other obstacles to the free flow of international trade offers another avenue of attack upon the problem. With positive national policies in operation designed to combine adaptation of costs and prices with maintenance of industrial activity, and with the exchange rates firmly held at agreed parities, action to remove many impediments to international commerce (quota and licensing systems, embargos, veterinary restrictions, arbitrary valuation systems, and other forms of indirect protection),[16] to simplify administrative procedures and regulations, to mitigate exchange controls, and to reduce tariffs could profitably be taken both unilaterally and by the negotiation of reciprocal trade agreements.

But it is important to be clear on one point. While the object of negotiations must be a general lowering

[16] *Cf.* P. W. Bidwell, *The Invisible Tariff* (New York, 1939).

of trade barriers, equilibrium cannot be reached by an equivalent lowering of all national trade barriers. The United States in particular cannot continue at one and the same time to have an agricultural surplus, a manufacturing export surplus, and a surplus of invisible exports such as shipping services and capital investment returning interest. The balance of payments must balance somehow. If its debtors are not to be forced into default on their interest payments and restrictions (by tariffs, import quotas, and exchange control) upon United States exports, this country must agree to accept larger imports. In order to do this, the tariff must be lowered appreciably upon certain agricultural products now produced at relatively high cost and upon a wide range of manufactured consumers' goods which at present are highly protected in the interest of small groups of producers. The logrolling that resulted in the Hawley-Smoot tariff schedules of 1930 protected a preposterous number of such items at small benefit to employment in the United States but with dire results both to the American consumer and to the foreign exporter. Unless these schedules can be drastically revised, the prospects of restoring a free multilateral trading system are remote.

That this revision will cause losses and hardships to the sectional interests concerned is a fact to be faced—no omelet can be made without some breaking of eggs. But these sectional interests are relatively small, and if, as has been postulated, American purchasing power is maintained at a high level, the difficulties of adjustment will be minimized. The major industries—those which provide the greatest volume of steady employment and the highest wages—would undoubtedly profit from such a policy.

The difficulties of removing protection from even the smallest groups are not to be underestimated in a democracy, but the powers granted to the Executive to negotiate reciprocal trade agreements run until 1943. The struggle for renewal of these powers will probably be decisive in regard not only to the tariff policy of the United States, but also in regard to the prospects of restoring free exchanges and multilateral trade in the world at large.

CHAPTER X

LONG-RUN OBJECTIVES

Wartime Centralization

THE greater part of the argument up to this point has necessarily been concerned with national economic policies in the short run. In order to carry through the immediate steps necessary to avert economic chaos in the years following the war, government policy must be directed toward price-cost adjustments without violent fluctuations of the general levels of prices and employment. This does not mean that centralized government control and operation is necessarily efficient in the economic field, even in the short run. There is, indeed, much evidence of waste and inefficiency in the conduct of hastily improvised agencies of government. Their personnel is rapidly assembled and not always well chosen. Relations between various agencies, and smooth delegation of authority within each agency, are not easy to organize hurriedly.

The direction of government calls for qualities different from those required in the management of private business or in academic life. Its tendency toward centralization creates confusion. The capital city of any country at war tends to become the chief bottleneck of production.

What makes government control inevitable at such a time is not any pre-eminent efficiency, but the necessity to subordinate normal economic activity to the strategic purposes of the government. Control is accepted, waste and inefficiency and confusion are tolerated, because there is one dominating purpose in the minds of all concerned, and that purpose can be achieved only by centralization of authority.[1]

It has been argued above that some wartime controls should be continued during the immediate postwar period. When the war ends, there will doubtless be large groups of people impatient of government control and fearful of its continuation. In some degree, their impatience will be justified by the incompetence and waste and doctrinaire tendencies of individuals or departments. In some degree it will arise from anxiety to get free of controls that inhibit short-run profit taking.

The tradition of individualism and private enterprise quickly reasserted itself, particularly in the

---

[1] *Cf.* Donald M. Nelson's speech to the National Association of Manufacturers. "To hell with this business of waiting to see how much it will cost. You get production going now and we will argue the terms and details as we go along. . . . Why not start inefficiently and figure out more efficient methods as you go along? Get the stuff moving and get it moving now!" *New York Times* (January 31, 1942), p. 9.

United States, after the last war. It may do so again.
It would be unfortunate if it did not revive.

In Europe also, it should not be forgotten, there is
widespread resentment against the harsh and detailed
regulation of private life that has been exercised by
totalitarian governments for many years. When those
governments are defeated, their methods will be dis-
credited with them. There may well be a great re-
vulsion against bureaucracy in all its forms. This
should be used to restore individual freedom in an
orderly framework.

Cautious Relaxation of Controls

Yet the reasons for caution in relaxing control of
economic activity during the transition period would
seem to be overwhelming. Some instruments of economic warfare should be rather quickly abolished before they become entrenched as new measures of
economic nationalism. Other controls should be maintained at least for a time.

In every country, belligerent or neutral, the strain
of war and the prospect of demobilization create a
highly unstable economic situation. Not only are there
likely to be production shortages and surpluses on a
great scale, but the distortion of economic effort is
masked by price and rationing controls, by government domination of the employment market, and gov-

ernment control of the money market. Potential disequilibria are not recognized so long as war controls are in operation; but their effect may be catastrophic if those controls are too suddenly removed. Every care should be taken to ward off two dangers: first, inflation, and then an aggravation of economic nationalism in the ensuing period of deflation.

Competitive enterprise, if left to follow normal profit incentives, might well cause a sudden outburst of purchasing as disastrous in its way as the equally sudden cessation of buying power that usually follows. In the confusion of price relationships that would thus be created, there is every prospect of the feverish speculation and accentuated disequilibria that are followed inevitably by a slump and devastating unemployment. To move abruptly from wartime control to a competitive peace economy would be to invite these disasters.

There is need for a cooling-off period, to get national economic activity gradually back toward more stable price-cost relations. This is the only way in which national disequilibria may be reduced and brought to manageable proportions. There is no escape from the necessity of adaptation. Prices and costs must be adjusted to peacetime instead of wartime demands.

The adjustment needed is that which would theoretically result from the free play of supply and demand, working toward competitive efficiency. The price system is no longer flexible enough to bring about such an equilibrium of competitive forces; but government policy must be directed to the same end if it is to maximize employment and national income.

The productive organization, price systems, and labor resources of most national economies were never adjusted to the changed international situation brought about by the last war. Indeed, it is only too clear that the maladjustments were aggravated by protective policies, so that the international market flew apart into fragmentary national markets.

A decade of totalitarian economics followed by years of economic warfare has gone far to complete the destruction of competitive economic equilibrium. Competition works effectively in smoothing out small irregularities in a well-established, stable, and highly organized market. In a disorganized market, where the irregularities are very great, its working is apt to be both violent and ineffective. Even though more people are now conscious of business cycles and wary of the temptation to make paper profits in a short-lived boom, the instability of the immediate postwar situation is likely to be too great to warrant premature relaxation of economic controls.

Account must also be taken of the political and psychological situation, as well as of the economic problems that will await solution. There may be little orderly organization remaining in many countries at the end of this war. Not only governments, but banking systems, monetary standards, business organization, law, and police regulation may need to be completely reorganized.

Moreover, if international relations are to be placed on a more stable and workable basis, there has to be a very considerable shift in responsibilities among the great powers. The United States, for example, does not have the banking and commercial organization adequate to the needs of a great creditor nation. It retains a high-tariff structure and many types of economic activity more appropriate to the circumstances prevailing half a century ago. It has also failed to provide itself with the institutions appropriate to its position as a great world power. Great Britain, on the contrary, may have to reduce its international establishment and overhead in view of its weakened economic situation. Every country has adaptations to make that cannot be hurried through in a brief period.

It is perhaps unnecessary to follow this line of argument any further. There is fairly general agreement among all but a few obstinate believers in the virtues of undiluted laissez faire that a period of transition is necessary.

A World Safe for Bureaucracy

Such agreement, however, ought not by implication to be construed as acceptance of government controls in their present forms as ideals to be striven for and defended. This is not a war to make the world safe for bureaucracy. There are some who dream of a completely cartelized world. Their plans, or blueprints, are structurally vague in detail, but grandiose in conception. If it is not likely that the world after the war can return to as large a measure of private enterprise as existed before 1939, it is even less likely that a completely planned world economy can be created, or if created, will prove efficient and acceptable in a democratic world. Autocratic and authoritarian controls have proved efficient for limited purposes when there has been a certain ruthlessness in their administration; but democratic discussion and executive efficiency in detailed planning do not go well together.

The function of the immediate postwar arrangements, therefore, should be to keep a potentially dangerous and even explosive situation under control until the danger of violent fluctuations of prices and employment is lessened. There is need for both national and international action. Some of the most effective efforts to free national economies in the period of exaggerated economic nationalism before the war—the Austrian relaxation of exchange control for example, the British conversion operations, and the Australian and Swedish combination of price-cost adjustment and monetary expansion that enabled those countries to emerge first from the 1929–32 depression—were carried through unilaterally.

Every opportunity should be taken to abolish specific production and price controls while retaining general control by means of monetary and fiscal policies. The replacement boom when the war ends may well provide an opportunity in many countries to get rid of much of the top-hamper of wartime regulation. If this opportunity is not taken, particular vested interests —among them the bureaucracies seeking to perpetuate their powers—may seek in the ensuing depression to saddle a mass of restrictive controls upon the community. The end result of such a development is the totalitarian state.

If this view prevails, it is more than ever necessary to keep long-run objectives and principles in mind while formulating plans for coping with immediate emergency problems. Some remedies are worse than the disease they are intended to cure; others alleviate symptoms but aggravate the basic causes of distress. Too many of the expedients adopted in the years between the wars fell into the latter category. Agrarian protection increased production in high-cost areas and diminished it in low-cost areas; subsidies increased surplus stocks that should have been disposed of even at a loss; thinly populated countries closed their doors to immigration and heavily populated countries subsidized marriage and childbirth. Creditor countries raised their tariff barriers.

No one can as yet project either the structure of a possible postwar world or the steps by which it can be achieved. The structure that will finally emerge from the unforeseen and unforeseeable developments of the years that lie ahead will certainly not be symmetrical and logical. The method of its creation will depend less upon international discussion and debate than upon political decisions as to national economic policy in the leading democratic countries.

It is, therefore, not an adequate solution, at this stage, to concentrate on the elaboration of plans for international institutions or fragments of world government. What matters most to the outside world as well as to Americans is the kind of fiscal, monetary, and investment policies combined with adjustments of costs and prices in private business that will be followed by American authorities, here, in the United States.

The orientation of public policy in the leading countries of the world toward improved nutrition, better housing, and more stable employment, which appears to be one of the goals to aim at, does not necessarily involve increased public administration and control over the whole field of economic activity. Indeed, there are cogent arguments for the separation rather than the blending of socialization and private enterprise. What is important is that the fields of co-operation shall be defined, and that each in its own field shall be developed according to its own particular characteristics and virtues. There is no necessary incompatibility between national policies of social security and free international trade.

Dangers of Regulated Trade

In the sphere of international economic relations, even more than in national economic policy, there is scope for a considerable measure of free enterprise. While bilateral purchasing agreements and multilateral commodity controls may be both wise and necessary over a transition period, this does not necessarily imply that such arrangements should be regarded as the beginnings of completely planned and regulated trade. Most of the international control schemes that have been operated or planned are confined to a relatively few simple and homogeneous foodstuffs or raw materials. A much greater variety of products, it is true, have been subject to international cartel arrangements; but the task of organizing world trade in all its variety is one to baffle the imagination.

What actually happens when control schemes are set up is that the production and trade in certain products are organized by those most directly interested— the producers. The efficiency of each organization is only too often judged with respect to the one product or group of products concerned. Only too often what results is government of producers, by producers, for producers. Even if consumer interests are able to assert themselves, there remains the problem of fitting the particular industry into the general economic situation.

It is relatively easy to subsidize both producers and consumers in a particular industry at the expense of the community as a whole. In the actual conduct of regulated trade there is always difficulty in accommodating the unusual and often small interests that add variety and richness of consumers' choice. Small producers are squeezed out, small consumers are disregarded, odd trades disappear.

The greatest risk to be run in any system of planned international trade, however, is the risk that it may quickly lose touch with any test of economic efficiency. The tendency is to freeze production and trade in their present patterns, to allot quotas on the basis of past production.

This is a very great risk to be run just now, when such profound disequilibria exist and have been aggravated by past controls. There is great need to discourage production in high-cost areas. Competitive trade would do so quickly and harshly. Controlled trade may, on the contrary, sustain and even expand production where it should be contracted. In the years before the war, wheatgrowers in many European countries were being subsidized heavily to produce wheat unprofitably at three times the price at which it could be produced in the United States where farmers were being paid not to grow wheat. Unless the interim controls projected after this war are designed to lead back toward freer competition among producing areas and among competing products, international trade may quickly come to be conducted by political rather than economic bargaining.

If this should happen, there is likely to be less beneficial exchange of goods, and increased friction between governments will result. The unfortunate results of mobilizing economic resources in totalitarian economic diplomacy ought by now to be sufficiently manifest. In such trade, every unpaid account or trade dispute becomes a diplomatic issue. Good relations even between friendly governments are not made any easier by such a development.

Moreover, any tendency to freeze the present pattern of productive specialization is to be deplored. Not the least value of international trade in the nineteenth century was its function as an agency of economic change and growth. It is difficult to envisage a system of controlled trade which could give scope for industrial development in backward areas and the opening up of new resources. But unless such developments can be encouraged, the uneven pressures of population increase in the modern world will surely provoke fresh explosions.

Exchange Stability

If neither uncontrolled laissez faire nor completely regulated trade can be envisaged as objectives to be aimed at in the interim period, it is possible to work toward a new framework of regulation within which trade may again proceed freely. Both national and international action are needed to establish such a framework. In every country, some reorientation of economic policy is necessary. Such reorientation (looking toward stabilization of production and employment within an international system of specialization) cannot, however, be achieved without international consultation and some measure of international discipline. The final justification for such policies can only be the achievement of competitive efficiency which was the objective by which price competition used to be justified, but which now seems unattainable by laissez faire methods.

It is necessary, therefore, to work toward exchange stabilization and the creation of international economic institutions for consultation and co-ordination, and ultimately for common supranational action. There is no justification in the modern world for autonomous national tariff policies or autonomous monetary policies. To free the exchanges suddenly during the difficult period that will follow the cessation of hostilities would be to risk disastrous capital flights and exchange depreciations. Indeed, the impoverished countries which will have need of large imports and even loans to replenish their resources must endeavor to avoid premature and perhaps uncontrollable depreciation of their currencies. As Professor Ellis has argued, also, in an address to the American Economic Association,[2] commodity prices must be kept down and inflationary tendencies controlled in the United States during this transition period. In the long run, however, the debtor countries must export in larger amounts to the United States, so that after the reconstruction period is past American prices should be relatively high.

It seems to be imperative, therefore, that some control of the exchanges must be maintained over the transition period; but during that period arrangements might well be made for stabilization of exchange rates at levels which will permit the controls to be removed gradually until trade can be conducted freely at equilibrium rates.

The establishment of any system for international consultation or action concerning national economic policies is fraught with difficulties. There is general agreement that selfish national policies, for example of competitive exchange depreciation or of tariff bargaining, tend to defeat their own purposes but in doing so involve heavy loss to other national communities. The anarchy of unfettered national sovereignties is widely criticized. It is often suggested that arrangements should be made calling for international consultation before tariffs are raised or exchange rates altered.

[2] Howard S. Ellis, "The Problem of Exchange Systems in the Postwar World" in *American Economic Review Supplement* (March, 1942), p. 202.

Such suggestions are open to the criticism that experience has shown that progress in restraining national governments from anarchic policies cannot be made merely by discussion. Supranational institutions with power to impose sanctions on offending countries must be created. In this view, an International Tariff Commission should have power to review, and if need be veto, changes in national tariffs, the sanction for defiance of its verdict being withdrawal of most-favored-nation treatment. In the same way, it is often suggested that authority to alter agreed exchange rates should be vested in an International Monetary Authority.

The difficulty about all such proposals is the old question—*quis custodiet custodes?* Who will constitute these international bodies? To whom will they be responsible? Whose interests will they watch?

The acid test of all such proposals is their application not to the little and weak countries but to the great and powerful.

The United States will in fact determine by its own actions what degree of international co-operation will be possible. Other countries, it must be repeated, will have little option or choice. Any limitations of sovereignty the United States is willing to accept, they will be almost bound to accept. If new international institutions are created in which the United States is an active member, there will be little difficulty in securing the adherence of other countries. If such institutions provide only means of consultation because the United States will not relinquish its autonomy in tariff and monetary policy, this is all that can be hoped for.

Such proposals as those suggested above clearly contemplate the establishment of supranational authority and steps toward a democratic world economy. They avoid the necessity of trying to create a complex and probably unworkable system of trade regulated in detail, and leave scope for a considerable measure of free-trading enterprise. But they involve the abandonment of anarchic and irresponsible nationalism.

The effectiveness of such measures will depend, however, upon the creation of political institutions for the preservation of peace. The possible form of such institutions is outside the scope of this book; but no discussion of economic questions would be realistic if it omitted such a reminder. The establishment of a stable economic order is impossible unless the forces of warlike aggression can be outlawed and disarmed.

CHAPTER XI

ILLUSION AND REALITY

THIS review of problems that must be faced and decisions that must be taken, if it is desired to restore the postwar world to some semblance of peaceful prosperity, does not cover all the issues; still less does it offer a complete and workable plan of action. No individual survey can do so. It is probable that solutions, if they come, will be hammered out by direct and laborious negotiations in which urgent practical necessities will force many compromises and concessions to temporary political pressures. No ideal solution is to be expected. Democracy stumbles toward its goals by a series of makeshift and unsatisfactory institutions and conventions. Those who work for the improvement of international relations have better cause than most people to know how far short of the ideal the best possible arrangement may fall. They must be content to aim high but to accept realistic practical arrangements that fall far short of their aim as long as some progress is made. Few with practical experience of the working of international politics retain any millennial illusions. The struggle for sanity in the relations between individuals and between states is long and disappointing.

It has gone on for centuries and will go on beyond our time.

There are many who recognize the need of action, but quail at the difficulties. Plans for international action are regarded as utopian. Their proponents, however cautious, are dubbed "starry-eyed idealists." National and local interests are thought to be too strong ever to be controlled in the common interest. If this is true, then the totalitarians are right. The alternative to international action is a resumption of the struggle for power. But democracy cannot be saved by giving up in defeat before trying to save it. Such defeatism ensures its own justification. No problem can be solved if it is put aside as insoluble.

It may be possible to construct in imagination a symmetrical scheme of international treaties and supranational institutions. Constitution making is a seductive occupation. But workable constitutions grow out of grimly felt necessities and are seldom symmetrical. That the nations will come again to the necessity of devising practical methods of world government is inevitable—if not after the painful lessons of this war, then after even sharper lessons in the future. After the last war there were some who struggled to put reality into the first attempt at the creation of organs of world government and perhaps more who put faith in them as a symbol. Some of those organs—the technical sections of the League, the International Labor Office, and the Bank for International Settlements—are still at work and will be used again. Any attempt to rebuild political institutions for international co-operation must surely be based also upon the experience gained at Geneva between the wars.

But government is a complex business, and any realistic attempt at the re-creation of organs of world government must do more than establish a skeleton organization with no power and small resources. The proliferation of national governments, the overlapping of many departments, the demarcation of central and local functions should indicate what is involved in an approach to world government. The problem may perhaps be stated as a sum in proportion: as Geneva was to Washington or even Ottawa, so was the efficiency of world to national organization. The task of rebuilding international institutions on a more solid and more adequate basis must be taken up again; but the digging of foundations is more important at present than the drawing of beautiful and elaborate plans.

It is assumed that the United Nations will win the war and retain in their own hands the power and the responsibility of enforcing world peace, and gradually bringing order out of the chaos of international economic relations. Upon this assumption it has been argued that the most important problems to be faced are those of national economic policy. For the successful prosecution of national economic policies aimed at higher living standards it is necessary to devise means of international co-ordination. The victorious nations must first of all fight against inflation and carry through measures of adjustment so as to achieve a balanced equilibrium in a peacetime economy. This will be most easily achieved if they can avoid the extremes of inflation and deflation.

Even the modest suggestions directed to this end entail very considerable responsibilities being shouldered by the democratic countries. Those responsibilities, at least for the United States, represent in many ways a sharp break with tradition and a bleak prospect of harassing involvement with the affairs of other peoples. During many decades of geographical isolation and absorption in the development of a continent, Americans have suffered little interference from the rest of the world and have had little desire to interfere with it.

It is therefore disconcerting for them to be confronted suddenly with a situation in which a substantial share of the responsibility for restoring order in a chaotic world is laid before a community that on the whole dislikes and distrusts Europe and all that it stands for of historic feuds and imperialist struggles for power. The impulse to disown any responsibility in the matter is quite natural, and there will be many who regard all suggestions concerning international co-operation as at best irresponsible and at worst a form of war propaganda.

The only reply to be made is that the world today is what modern science has made it, a community or neighborhood closer-knit than was the little group of colonies that banded itself together to form the United States a hundred and sixty-odd years ago. An American listener can now hear, daily, eyewitness reports of happenings in the most distant areas of the globe: business or political envoys can fly to those areas faster than the founding fathers could travel from one end of their new country to the other. In his daily life, the average American rolls on Javanese rubber, in an automobile strengthened by Chinese tungsten, and incorporating over 180 materials, many of which come from outside the United States. The telephone system he uses is built with chromium from Rhodesia, cobalt from the Congo, nickel from Canada, antimony from China, tin from Malaya, rubber from the East Indies, silk from Japan, varnish from New Zealand kauri gum and Chinese tung oil, carnauba wax from Brazil, Manila hemp from the Philippines, jute from India, shellac from Siam. The realities of international economic relations are with us throughout our daily life.[1] It is an illusion to believe that we can isolate ourselves from them.

[1] Cf. *International Economic Relations*, Report of the Commission of Inquiry into National Policy (University of Minnesota Press, 1934), p. 17: "We need only make mention of drugs derived from tropical plants like quinine, cocaine, and ipecac; of tropical spices and flavoring materials like pepper, cloves, mace, allspice, vanilla, and ginger; of certain tropical woods like teak, mahogany, and ebony; of certain hides, skins, and furs derived from animals neither indigenous to nor domesticated in the United States; of works of art; of handicraft products like Oriental and Chinese

They are, unfortunately, inextricably tangled with the problem of peace. If the advantages of international trade and communications could be obtained without the necessity of assuring peaceful security, the world would be a simpler place. No one wants to see his country go to war, but as Mr. R. H. Tawney has recently reminded us, "it is possible that not the least guilty among the authors of war were those of us who desired only to be let alone to live in peace." The utilization of the world's resources cannot be dissociated from the necessity for keeping order in the world. Moreover, no individual or community can ever escape the responsibility that goes with power. The United States is the most powerful community in the modern world. The responsibility of its citizens is an inescapable function of that power.

---

rugs, hand-made laces, and hand embroideries; of precious stones like diamonds, rubies, emeralds, and sapphires not found in appreciable volume in the United States; of unmanufactured rattan and bamboo; of foreign language books, maps, and prints; of nickel and cobalt; of platinum essential in our laboratories and in our chemical and electrical industries; of kauri, copal, and lac for varnishes; of chicle, tragacanth, and kadaya gums; of special foods like Brazil and cashew nuts, smoked sturgeon, bananas, limes and lime juice, special types of cheeses not produced in the United States, and out-of-season fruits from the antipodes; of many types of tanning material (e. g., quebracho and mangrove) to supplement our dwindling supplies of oak bark, and tanning extracts from our vanishing chestnut and hemlock forests; of sisal, Manila hemp, and other tropical fibers."

INDEX

Agrarian reform in Europe, 123
Agricultural protectionism, and international economic equilibrium, 103 ff., 114 ff.; in Germany, 117 ff.; in the United States, 125 f.
Agricultural surpluses, 103 ff., 109 f.; control of, 110 f.
Atlantic Charter, 53, 63 ff., 82, 85 n., 124, 189, 200

Bank for International Settlements, 59 n., 81, 91 n., 147 n.
Beveridge, Sir William, 60 n.
Bidwell, P. W., 204 n.
Bland, R. L., see Surface, F. M.
Board of Economic Warfare, 57 f.
Brandt, Karl, 108 n.
British-American economic relations, 200 ff.
Brodie, H. B., and Kapp, K. W., 50 n.
Bulletin of International News, 202 n.
Burke, Edmund, 160

Callis, Helmut G., 176 n.
Carnegie Endowment for International Peace, 36, 62 n.
Central European bloc, formation of, 70
China, reconstruction in, 173; League of Nations technical aid to, 180 f.
Chinese Banking Consortium, 174 f.
Churchill, Winston S., 53, 64, 65
Clémentel, Etienne, 59
Cobden Treaty, 193
Commercial policy, problems of postwar, 46 f., 189 ff.; of the United States, 145, 192, 199 ff., 205 f.; of Great Britain, 200 ff.
Conard, Joseph, 184 n.
Condliffe, J. B., 88 n., 107 n., 198 n.
Consumption levels, improvement of, 170 ff.
Co-operation, wartime economic, 55 ff.
Credit policies, co-ordination of, 100 f.
Crowther, Geoffrey, 61 n., 95 n., 98 n., 143, 161 n., 202 n.

Das, R. K., 170
Davidson, Sir Alfred, 198 n.
Dearle, N. B., 50 n.
Department of State Bulletin, 57 n., 64 n., 157 n.
Direct investment, 178

Economic adaptation, 89 ff., 213; and regulated trade, 217 f.

Economic conditions after 1918, 85 ff.
Economic demobilization, 32 ff., 47 ff., 89 ff., 132 ff., 136 ff.
Economic mobilization, 133 f.
Economic nationalism, 34, 193
Economic policy, postwar, 59
Economic progress, and population growth, 171
Economic self-sufficiency, 190 f.
Economic warfare, 28, 194
Economist, 155 n., 201 n.
Ellis, H. S., 198 n., 199, 220
Employment, maintenance of, 91 ff., 139 ff.
Evian Conference, 183, 187
Exchange control, 197 ff., 201, 219 f.
Exchange stabilization, 146 ff., 202 ff., 218 ff.

Field, F. V., 174 n.
Foreign Agriculture, 110 n.
Fortune, 48 n., 49 n., 140 n.
Free trade in the nineteenth century, 191 f.

Germany, agricultural protectionism in, 117 ff.
Gerschenkron, Alexander, 117 n.
Gold standard after 1918, 87
Government regulation, in wartime, 194 f., 207 ff.; in the transition period, 197 ff., 208, 212 ff.; relaxation of, 209 ff.; and private enterprise, 215
Great Britain, public debt in, 135; international economic position of, 143 f., 154 ff., 200 ff., 212; commercial policy of, 200 ff.

Hall, N. F., 130 n., 138 n., 147 n.
Hansen, A. H., 168 n.
Harris, S. E., 132 n., 154 n., 202 n.
Hobson, O. R., 169 n.
Hogben, Lancelot, 190 n.
Holland, W. L., 73 n.
Hoover, Herbert, 60
Hoover moratorium, 152
Hope-Simpson, Sir John, 184 n.
Horsfall, P., 32 n.
Howland, C. P., 179 n.
Hull, Cordell, 199
Huxley, Julian, 67 n.

Inflation, 49 ff., 134 f.
Inter-Allied Agreement, September, 1941, 53 f., 182
Inter-Allied collaboration after 1918, 49 f., 58 ff.
Inter-Allied Review, 54 n.
Inter-American Coffee Agreement, 112 f.
Inter-American Jewish Conference, 183
International Chamber of Commerce, 36, 88 n.
International commodity controls, 111 ff., 216 f.
International economic co-operation, 61, 81 ff., 218 ff.; failure to achieve, 34 ff.; political basis of, 62 ff.; and national employment policies, 94 f.; and national credit policies, 100 f.; United States and, 221 f., 226 ff.
International economic equilibrium, and social security, 88 f.; restoration of, 89 ff.; and agricultural protectionism, 103 ff., 114 ff.; and national economic policies, 124 f., 145 ff.

International Economic Relations, 227 n.

International investment, after 1918, 174, 177 f.; new frontiers of, 167 ff.; in the nineteenth century, 173 f.; new forms of, 173 ff.; the state and, 177

International Labor Conference, 66, 70, 81 f.

International monetary co-operation, 146 f., 202 f., 218 ff.

International Wheat Agreement, July, 1941, 113

Journal of Farm Economics, 102 n.

Kapp, K. W., *see* Brodie, H. B.
Keynes, J. M., 136 n., 155 n., 203 n.

Lausanne Conference, 153
League of Nations, 31, 106, 108 n., 109 n., 117 n., 128 n., 129 n., 144, 171 n., 181 n.; loans of, 176, 179 f.; technical aid of, 179, 180 ff.

Lease-lend agreements, 157 ff., 189
Lease-lend aid, 54 f., 112, 154 ff.

McDougall, F. L., 130, 131
Miller, Douglas, 133 n., 195 n.
Most-favored-nation treatment, 192
Moulton, H. G., and Pasvolsky, Leo, 152 n.

National economic policies, and international economic equilibrium, 124 f., 145 ff.
"National Minimum," 97
National sovereignty, limitation of, 67 n., 124 f.

National treatment, 192
Nelson, D. M., 208 n.
Neutrality Act, 154
New York Times, 54 n., 67 n., 70 n., 98 n., 112 n., 123 n., 155 n., 177 n., 183 n., 200 n., 208 n.
Nine-Power Pact, 76 f.
Nishihara loans, 175
Nutrition policy, 126 ff.

"Open door," the, 192
Orr, John Boyd, 127, 128 n.

Pasvolsky, Leo, *see* Moulton, H. G.
Peace settlement, problems of a, 44 ff.
Population growth and economic progress, 171
Postwar planning in the United States, 57 f.
Prince, D. C., 140 n.
Private enterprise, and social security, 98 f.; and government control, 215
Prokopovicz, S. N., 172 n.
Public debt, in Great Britain, 135; in the United States, 135; composition of, 138
Public works, 92 f., 139

Rajchmann, Dr. L., 55 n.
Rappard, W. E., 35 n.
Raw materials, access to, 189 ff.
Refugee settlement, 179, 183 ff.
Regionalism, in Europe, 67 ff.; in the Far East, 73 ff.; in the Western Hemisphere, 78 ff.; limitations of, 77 ff.
Relief, organization of, 30
Remer, C. F., 176 n.

Reparations, 150 ff., 162 ff.
Replacement boom, 137
Roosevelt, Franklin D., 53, 63, 66, 82, 156
Röpke, Wilhelm, 117 n.

Sforza, Carlo, 123 n.
Shanghai, Japanese operations on the exchange market, 195 f.
Simpson, Smith, 98 n.
Social security, 82 f., 85 ff., 95 ff.; and international economic equilibrium, 88 f.; and private enterprise, 98 f.; the development of, 102 f.
"Stagnation thesis," 168 f.
Staley, Eugene, 50, 51, 56 n., 77, 78, 199 n.
Sun Yat-sen, 173
Supranational institutions, 83, 219, 221, 224 f.
Surface, F. M., and Bland, R. L., 50 n., 59 n.

Tasca, Henry J., 200 n.
Tawney, R. H., 37 n., 40, 46 n., 228
Taxation, 135 f.
Temperley, H. W. V., 50 n., 59 n.
Temporary National Economic Committee, 168 n.
Timoshenko, V. P., 106 n.
Totalitarian trading policies, 195 ff.

Totalitarianism, the challenge of, 38 ff.
Toynbee, A. J., 37 n., 95 n., 193 n.
Trade, regulation of, 194 f., 216 ff.
Trade barriers, removal of, 204 ff.
Transition period, 29, 48 f., 66, 80; government regulation in the, 197 ff., 208, 212 ff., 219 ff.
Tripartite Agreement, 147, 203

U.S.S.R., relations with the, 41 f., 172, 176 f.
United States, postwar planning in the, 57 f.; loans to Europe by the, 87, 177 f.; agricultural protectionism in the, 125 f.; public debt in the, 135; maintenance of employment in the, 142 f.; international economic position of the, 144 f., 212; commercial policy of the, 145, 192, 199 f., 205 f.; and international economic co-operation, 221 f., 226 ff.

Waight, Leonard, 147 n.
Walker, E. R., 136 n.
War debts, 150 ff.
Welles, Sumner, 183, 200 n.
Wheeler, L. A., 109 n., 112 n., 113 n.
Wickard, C. R., 112 n.
Wright, Quincy, 49 n.